IMPROVING COLLEGE ADMISSION TEST SCORES
Verbal Workbook

Jay Comras
Jeffrey Zerowin

National Association of Secondary School Principals
Reston, Virginia 22091

Jay Comras is supervisor of language arts
for Fair Lawn Public Schools, Fair Lawn,
New Jersey, and Jeffrey Zerowin is assistant principal at Park West High School,
New York City.

They acknowledge the contributions of
Gerald Giemzo, Ilona Mellor, Jeffrey K.
Smith, Ph.D., and Eleanor Weiner.
Project consultant was Frank J.
Montalbano and text consultants were
Kathryn Beam, Ph.D. and David Geiger,
Ph.D.

Produced by NASSP's editorial office:
Thomas F. Koerner, editor, and Eugenia
C. Potter, project editor.

National Association of Secondary School Principals
1904 Association Drive, Reston, Virginia 22091

TABLE OF CONTENTS

Foreword

The purpose of this workbook is to improve your competency with certain important verbal skills, the kinds of skills that are examined in college admission tests such as the SAT. The workbook, and the attendant videotapes, will also develop your familiarity with the testing formats used for the SAT. An improvement in (or review of) abstract verbal skills and an acquaintance with testing formats can raise your scores on the SAT and similar college admission examinations.

The SAT measures *trained* aptitudes, not simply "raw intelligence." It probes not only your reasoning ability and capacity for abstract concepts, but also explores your vocabulary and reading competencies. In part, it gauges how well you have *applied in school and out of school* the mental capabilities that you possess.

The exercises in this verbal workbook cannot substitute for years of solid class work. They can, however, enhance prior schoolwork as well as correct some deficiencies that you may possess but currently do not recognize. So, use this workbook as a diagnostic key and as a refresher and review program.

Finally, we wish you the best of success on examination day. Be sure to get a good sleep the night before and have confidence in your preparation and in yourself.

Scott D. Thomson
Executive Director
NASSP

Introduction

The questions in the SAT are designed to measure a variety of verbal skills that are classified by item type and by degree of difficulty. The content is diverse and the questions are carefully chosen to avoid ethnic or cultural bias.

The antonyms, analogies, and sentence completion questions are referred to as *discrete* items; that is, they are separate and distinct in themselves. The vocabulary words in discrete items are classified in one of four categories: aesthetic—philosophical, the world of practical affairs, science, or human relations. Some require only a general understanding while other words require a fine distinction. The reading comprehension questions are not discrete because they are associated with the reading comprehension passages. These passages are selected from: narrative writing, argumentative writing, the humanities, social studies, physical science, and biological science. The reading levels vary from eleventh grade high school to second year college. The questions require the student: to recognize the main idea, to identify supporting details, to make inferences, to analyze arguments, to recognize the tone or attitude of the writer, and to make generalizations.

The Test of Standard Written English evaluates basic principles of grammar, usage, diction, and idiom as well as more complex writing problems such as logical comparison, sentence construction, and punctuation.

This NASSP program is based upon a thorough analysis of questions found in SAT examinations. It is designed to refresh basic skills and review test-taking strategies.

Orientation

INTRODUCTION TO THE SAT

The Scholastic Aptitude Test is a multiple-choice test that is designed to provide colleges with a broad estimate of a student's academic ability. It is used in combination with a student's high school record in making admissions decisions. The SAT currently consists of three separate subtests: the Verbal subtest, which measures verbal reasoning ability, vocabulary, and reading comprehension; the Mathematics subtest, which measures mathematical reasoning ability in the areas of arithmetic, algebra, and geometry; and the Test of Standard Written English (TSWE), which measures knowledge of grammar, punctuation, and sentence construction.

There are six sections on the SAT: two Verbal, two Mathematics, one TWSE, and one experimental section. The experimental section is used in the development of new tests and does not count in the scoring. This section will contain questions in one of the three subtest areas; it will not be identified as experimental, so students must take each section seriously. The number of items on each section will vary, but the time limit is a strictly enforced 30 minutes.

The SATs are designed to measure a wide range of ability. Consequently some of the items are very difficult while others are fairly easy. It is important for students not to become discouraged when the test gets hard.

Many students take the SATs more than once in hopes of improving their scores the second time around. Students should note that all scores are sent to colleges, not just the highest set. Therefore, it is probably not wise to approach taking the SATs in a "just-for-practice" frame of mind.

Colleges vary substantially in the degree to which they consider SAT scores in making admission decisions. Some colleges do not require them at all; at other schools they are the single most important factor in admissions. The SAT represents a singular intellectual challenge to high school students. A background of strong academic courses taken in high school combined with a diligent effort in preparation for the test will enable the student to meet this challenge successfully.

HOW TO USE THE VERBAL SERIES

The verbal series consists of an orientation section, five verbal lessons,* two lessons in preparation for the Test of Standard Written English, and a full-length (85 question) simulated SAT Verbal Examination. These lessons are designed to build self-confidence, refresh cognitive skills, and give you practice in working with test questions.

Each of the five lessons contains four sections.

The first section is an abridged simulated examination. This is a timed test that is divided into four segments: opposites, sentence completion, analogies, and reading comprehension. You are allowed 30 minutes for the entire test, and you should time yourself. Be sure to follow the instructions in each segment. Mark your answers on the appropriate answer sheet printed in the back of the book. The answers, along with an explanation, will be given to you by your classroom teacher or will be reviewed in the corresponding televised lesson.

The second section is a skill builder. The skill builder will focus on some aspect of the SAT and is designed to reinforce the essential skills often found in the examination. Follow the instructions and complete the entire assignment. The answers, along with an explanation, will be given to you by your classroom teacher or will be reviewed in the corresponding televised lesson.

*referred to in the video series as booklets or units.

The third section is a vocabulary builder. The vocabulary builder employs methods advocated by some of America's leading educators. Each of the vocabulary builder sections focuses upon: (1) acquiring a core of essential words, (2) learning important prefixes, roots, and suffixes, (3) acquiring the meanings of words from context, (4) studying etymology, and (5) examining a word's denotative and connotative values. The vocabulary builder is designed to develop important cognitive skills. Follow the instructions and complete all of the exercises. The answers will be reviewed by your classroom teacher.

The fourth section is a vocabulary check test. Take the check test only when you have completed the exercises in the vocabulary builder. The answers, along with an explanation, will be given to you by your classroom teacher or will be reviewed in the corresponding televised lesson.

SIMULATED TEST OF STANDARD WRITTEN ENGLISH

Tests I and II

The Test of Standard Written English is a separate 30-minute examination that measures your ability to use acceptable appropriate written English. This test does *not* affect your score on the SAT. You receive a separate and independent score that is used to assist colleges in choosing an English program that is best for you. The test is divided into three sections: (I) 25 usage questions, (II) 15 sentence correction questions, and (III) 10 usage questions. The answers, along with an explanation, will be given to you by your classroom teacher or will be reviewed in the corresponding televised lesson. Mark your answers on the appropriate answer sheet printed in the back of the book. Students are encouraged to seek advice and/or assistance from their teachers regarding the many writing skills being evaluated. The purpose of the two tests is to assist you in identifying your strengths and weaknesses. You should use a reputable grammar and writing textbook to review basic principles.

FULL LENGTH, SIMULATED SAT VERBAL EXAMINATION

Section 1 .... 45 questions
Section 2 .... 40 questions

The purpose of this examination is to provide you with an opportunity to review the skills and test-taking strategies that you have learned. Each section takes 30 minutes to complete. Mark your answers on the appropriate answer sheet printed in the back of the book. The answers, along with an explanation, will be given to you by your classroom teacher or will be reviewed in the corresponding televised lesson.

SCORING THE SIMULATED EXAMINATIONS

Since these are simulated tests, they are not intended to correlate with performance on actual College Entrance Examinations. These tests are designed to build self-confidence and to give you practice in working with test questions. Your score may or may not be indicative of your performance in real situations.

SCORING FORMULA

| Number Right | (Minus) | ¼ Number Wrong | = | Raw Score |

NOTE: Questions that are *not* attempted or
answered are *not* counted as right or wrong.

SIMULATED CONVERSION TABLE
(Raw Score)

40 QUESTION TEST		45 QUESTION TEST	
1-5	200-270	1-5	200-270
6-10	280-350	6-10	280-320
11-15	360-410	11-15	330-380
16-20	420-480	16-20	390-440
21-25	490-550	21-25	450-500
26-30	560-620	26-30	510-560
31-35	630-690	31-35	570-620
36-40	700-800	36-40	630-680
		41-45	690-800

REMEMBER: THESE SCORES ARE NOT INDICATIVE OF YOUR ACTUAL PERFORMANCE. SCORES ON EACH OF THESE TESTS WILL VARY BECAUSE OF DIFFERENCES IN DIFFICULTY AND COMPOSITION FREQUENCY.

READING COMPREHENSION

Two paragraphs are listed below. These paragraphs will be used by your classroom teacher to introduce the reading comprehension sections.

Paragraph #1
"The raising of Japanese babies is the antithesis of Western child-rearing methods. In the United States we immediately prove to the baby that his wishes are not the only ones to be considered. Feeding and sleeping schedules attest to this. In addition, certain foods are not permitted and certain behaviors are punished. In Japan, however, maximum freedom is allowed to babies. Firm disciplines are non-existent for babies and are actually applied only at the beginning of adolescence."

* * * * * * * * * * * *

Express the main idea in your own words:

_____

_____

Paragraph #2
"Social custom, fear of losing their femininity, and the appeal of a social life have been given as reasons for the paucity of women who make athletics a career. No doubt these explanations have some validity. However, the lack of opportunities to participate in professional sports may be a more important factor. Of the 21 professional sports registered by the National Sports Federation of America, only 2 are certified as sports in which professional women athletes may compete. When the National Women's Sports Association, a group representing amateur athletes, asked to be a part of the Federation, the vote was overwhelmingly in favor of their exclusion."

* * * * * * * * * * * *

Express the main idea in your own words:

_____

_____

Verbal
Lesson
One

Simulated Verbal Examination

Time—30 Minutes

(The answers to the examination will be reviewed in televised Verbal Lesson One or by your classroom teacher.)

Segment 1: Opposites

Select the word that is most nearly opposite in meaning to the word or phrase in capital letters. Consider any fine shades of meaning that may exist.

Example:

HOT: (A) green   (B) river   (C) cold
        (D) above   (E) sweet

A	B	C	D	E
○	○	●	○	○

1. INJURIOUS: (A) savage   (B) beneficial   (C) petty
                  (D) delicate   (E) cheerful

2. CULTIVATE: (A) corrupt   (B) chop   (C) neglect
                  (D) pour   (E) accumulate

3. SPOIL: (A) prove   (B) exude   (C) succeed
                  (D) sour   (E) enrich

4. SENSIBLE: (A) indecent   (B) suspicious   (C) ironic
                  (D) foolish   (E) observant

5. NERVELESS: (A) fearless   (B) considerate   (C) silly
                  (D) abusive   (E) overjoyed

6. LINGER: (A) increase   (B) stabilize   (C) prolong
                  (D) hasten   (E) save

7. RECONCILE: (A) clutter   (B) alienate   (C) embroil
                  (D) close   (E) vex

8. VEHEMENT: (A) veracious   (B) forcible   (C) subdued
                  (D) unimportant (E) viable

9. ENUMERATE: (A) implore   (B) sample   (C) mass
                  (D) galvanize   (E) fall short

10. DUBIOUS: (A) impervious (B) useless   (C) decisive
                  (D) pious   (E) potent

1

11. PLIANT: (A) indirect   (B) strange   (C) obvious
                        (D) unbending   (E) effete

12. PARABLE: (A) invention   (B) stigma   (C) literalness
                        (D) magnificence (E) inversion

13. COPIOUSNESS: (A) discrepancy (B) paucity   (C) monopoly
                        (D) displeasure (E) calumny

14. CHIC: (A) elegant   (B) dated   (C) tricky
                        (D) menial   (E) disagreeable

15. ASCETIC: (A) flagellant   (B) demagog   (C) glutton
                        (D) atheist   (E) clairvoyant

Segment 2: Sentence Completion

The blanks in each sentence indicate omitted words. Select the word or words that best fit the meaning of the entire sentence and should be inserted in the blank.

Example:

On a small farm in an arid climate one should not grow crops that need considerable _____

or _____ to ripen.

(A) fertilizer — attention   (B) space — water
(C) sun — air   (D) tilling — harvesting
(E) weeding — insecticides

                                           A   B   C   D   E
                                         ○   ●   ○   ○   ○

---

16. Much of the midwestern American countryside is remarkably _____, producing abundant

crops and containing ample nutrients.

(A) torrid   (B) overflowing
(C) wealthy   (D) fertile
(E) primeval

17. For years it has been a _____ to grant foreign service officers an expense account for the _____

of moving abroad.

(A) policy — trouble   (B) rule — assignment
(C) tradition — cost   (D) technique — alienation
(E) way — indignation

18. In spite of increasing revenues, after seven years of continuous _____ spending the company

went into _____.

(A) controlled — reorganization   (B) regulated — black ink
(C) audited — acquisitions   (D) investment — marketing
(E) deficit — bankruptcy

19. Because interest rates are too _____, housing construction tends to be _____.

(A) flexible — regionalized   (B) unstable — seasonal
(C) high — curtailed   (D) expensive — increased
(E) depressed — inflationary

2

20. Unlike certain species, man's strategy for survival has not been specialization but _____, for we can farm, travel, build, and think.
    (A) diversification
    (B) uniformity
    (C) domestication
    (D) management
    (E) evolvement

21. A psychologist analyzes the _____ of an author; a _____ analyzes the character of his handwriting.
    (A) thoughts — lexicographer
    (B) words — teacher
    (C) personality — graphologist
    (D) language — critic
    (E) symbolism — connoisseur

22. For some, violence on television may be a way of _____ working off _____ by means of fantasy.
    (A) forcibly — guilt
    (B) vicariously — aggression
    (C) innocently — evil
    (D) grotesquely — hate
    (E) pleasurably — unnatural desires

23. It is extremely unreasonable to expect any child to _____ in life if he is _____ the opportunity of an education.
    (A) succeed — denied
    (B) labor — provided
    (C) find satisfaction — pondering
    (D) be opinionated — given
    (E) reason — rejecting

24. The greyhound has always been noted for its _____; the tortoise for its _____.
    (A) promptness — grotesqueness
    (B) sagacity — docility
    (C) swiftness — languor
    (D) stamina — aggressiveness
    (E) stature — agility

25. The surface of the earth is uniquely _____: it produces our food, provides our basic fuels, and supports our concrete structures.
    (A) prodigious
    (B) versatile
    (C) prolific
    (D) dissimilar
    (E) assiduous

Segment 3: Analogies

Each question below contains a related pair of words or phrases followed by five lettered pairs of words or phrases. Select the answer that best expresses a relationship similar to that expressed in the original pair.

Example:

PURSUE: CATCH::

(A) occur: happen
(B) eat: drink
(C) track: overtake
(D) apprehend: chase
(E) contest: victory

                                          A   B   C   D   E
                                            ○   ○   ●   ○   ○

26. ESTATE: FRONTAGE::

   (A) yard: campus
   (B) beach: strand
   (C) oasis: desert
   (D) rock: clay
   (E) ranch: farm

27. FLAVOR: TASTE::

   (A) cassette: hear
   (B) mirror: see
   (C) texture: touch
   (D) calculator: count
   (E) stove: eat

28. OCEAN: MARITIME::

   (A) polar: frigid
   (B) Earth: atlas
   (C) freighter: steamship
   (D) fish: piscatorial
   (E) celestial: moon

29. HOOP: BARREL::

   (A) wall: studs
   (B) binding: book
   (C) nail: birch
   (D) hoe: garden
   (E) pipe: derrick

30. ELOQUENT: CONVINCING::

   (A) fluent: awkward
   (B) verbose: pithy
   (C) loquacious: solemn
   (D) effusive: talkative
   (E) gabby: dumb

31. SULTRY: SUMMER::

   (A) chilly: winter
   (B) bleak: fall
   (C) thawing: spring
   (D) timely: season
   (E) bronzed: sunshine

32. DRAKE: COLT::

   (A) stallion: vixen
   (B) filly: cow
   (C) gelding: filly
   (D) hart: bull
   (E) sow: boar

33. PARADOX: CONTRADICTION::

   (A) inherent: unavoidable
   (B) mimicry: imitation
   (C) desideratum: decision
   (D) fidelity: surety
   (E) audible: tactile

34. BIOLOGIST: ELECTRON MICROSCOPE::

   (A) surgeon: scalpel
   (B) dentist: examination
   (C) compass: navigator
   (D) lawyer: court
   (E) engineer: calculator

35. AFICIONADO: ART::

   (A) musician: violin
   (B) soldier: war
   (C) Crete: El Greco
   (D) ivory: carving
   (E) partisan: group

4

Segment 4: Reading Comprehension

The questions following each passage are based on its content. Your choice should be made on the basis of what is stated or implied in the passage.

The U.S. campaign in Cuba lasted 10 weeks, killed 5,000 Americans (fewer than 400 dying of battle wounds), involved an invasion force of 18,000 men, and cost approximately $250,000,000. It caused comparatively little destruction of the Cuban populace or their property. The Philippine Insurrection lasted 2 years, killed 4,000 Americans (again most non-battle-connected), involved an invasion force of 65,000 troops, and cost over $600,000,000. It wreaked a huge amount of destruction causing death from malnutrition, disease, and slaughter of 200,000 civilians and 20,000 Filipino soldiers.

Whereas our imperialist venture in the "splendid little war" with Spain, over almost before it began, evoked comparatively little anti-imperialist sentiment among the American people, our pacification and occupation of the Philippines were accompanied by a very significant outpouring of anti-imperialist and anti-war sentiment.

Why then, I wondered, has so little space been devoted to the far costlier, and in its day, well-publicized conflict? Why, in the history books, only vague, generalized, sparse summarizations of such a traumatic experience in our history? Was it lack of interest or could it have been, as some have charged, an attempt to gloss over a less than glorious episode in the nation's history?

Moreover, I was struck by the many similarities between the Filipino insurgency at the turn of the century and the recent, unhappy conflict in Vietnam. Both involved areas in the Far East inhabited by so-called backward people, against whom the U.S. was clearly the aggressor. In both instances the U.S. assumed the role of a former imperialist power. In both cases there were factions at home who supported the U.S. policy, and partisans, who participated in strong anti-war movements. Both conflicts were marked by racism, atrocities, guerilla warfare, pious statements of policy defenders, and numerous promises of victory just around the corner. Both "rebel" leaders, Aguinaldo and Ho-Chi Minh, were regarded as moderates among their cohorts, and both made peace overtures to the opposing western forces. Most terrible

5

of all, both were marked by a tremendous degree of human and material destruction, although the U.S. did not have then the capacity of such devastation as it was to
55 have later.

There were also differences. The physical acquisition and possession of land were dominating influences among imperialists of the 19th and early 20th centuries, but they were not
60 factors in the Vietnam escapade in which Americans simply wanted to make the area safe from Communism. Both conflicts were led by wily, dedicated patriots: Aguinaldo, a young man of 30, proved to be unsuccessful in
65 his attempt to fulfill his goal of independence and upon his capture, he was forced to sign an oath of allegiance to the U.S. Ho-Chi Minh, an elderly leader, although he did not live to see his forces victorious, saw them well on
70 their way to this objective.

The Vietnamese War was longer, costlier, infinitely more destructive than the Philippine one, and, in the end, the U.S. was compelled to call it quits, despite the over-
75 whelming number of men and amount of material that it poured into the area. The Vietnamese, more grimly determined than the Filipinos, proved to be better tacticians, better disciplined and trained, and, there-
80 fore, a more deadly foe. The Viet Cong were more united, and displayed a singleness of purpose, whereas the Filipinos, composed of many different nationalities and groups, were often divided by quarrels, dis-
85 putes, old antagonisms, and jealousies.

36. According to the passage, which of the following is (are) true of both the Philippine Insurrection and the Vietnam War?

   I.   Both campaigns are treated inadequately in history books
   II. In both campaigns the acquisition of land was an objective of the U.S.
   III. Each resulted in massive deaths to the inhabitants

   (A) I only   (B) II only
   (C) III only   (D) I and III only
   (E) II and III only

37. The author feels that in comparison to the Philippine Insurrection, Americans viewed the Cuban campaign as being

   (A) More ferocious   (B) More costly
   (C) More popular   (D) More inglorious
   (E) More unsuccessful

38. The author suggests that victory in war is closely related to

   (A) The tenacity of a people   (B) The size of the civilian population
   (C) The size of the military force   (D) The dedication of its leaders
   (E) The pursuit of noble objectives

39. The author is primarily interested in describing

    (A) The effects of military discipline and training
    (B) Similarities among wars in the Far East
    (C) Imperialist and anti-imperialist campaigns
    (D) Analogous and dissimilar relationships in military conflicts
    (E) The devastating effects of war

40. The author employs all of the following except

    (A) Contrast   (B) Documentation
    (C) Statistics   (D) Illustration
    (E) Emphasis

But a man must keep an eye on his servants, if he would not have them rule him. Man is a shrewd inventor and is ever taking the hint of a new machine from his own structure,
5 adapting some secret of his own anatomy in iron, wood and leather to some required function in the work of the world. But it is found that the machine unmans the user. What he gains in making cloth, he loses in general
10 power. There should be temperance in making cloth, as well as in eating. A man should not be a silk-worm, nor a nation a tent of caterpillars. The robust rural Saxon degenerates in the mills to the Leicester stockinger,
15 to the imbecile Manchester spinner—far on the way to be spiders and needles. The incessant repetition of the same hand-work dwarfs the man, robs him of his strength, wit and versatility, to make a pin-polisher, a
20 buckle-maker, or any other specialty; and presently, in a change of industry, whole towns are sacrificed like ant-hills, when the fashion of shoestrings supersedes buckles, when cotton takes the place of linen, or railways of turn-
25 pikes, or when commons are enclosed by landlords. Then society is admonished of the mischief of the division of labor, and that the best political economy is care and culture of men; for in these crises all are ruined except
30 such as are proper individuals, capable of thought and of new choice and the application of their talent to new labor. Then again come in new calamities. England is aghast at the disclosure of her fraud in the adulteration
35 of food, of drugs and of almost every fabric in her mills and shops; finding that milk will not nourish, nor sugar sweeten, nor bread satisfy, nor pepper bite the tongue, nor glue stick. In true England all is false and forged.
40 This too is the reaction of machinery, but of the larger machinery of commerce. 'Tis not, I suppose, want of probity, so much as the tyranny of trade, which necessitates a per-

7

petual competition of underselling, and that
45 again a perpetual deterioration of the fabric.
(Ralph Waldo Emerson, *English Traits*)

41. Which of the following best describes the content of the passage?

  (A) An analysis of events that led to England's economic downfall
  (B) A philosophical account of the dangers of industrialization
  (C) An explanation of change in society
  (D) A revelation of the inadequacy of man's talents
  (E) An account of economic prosperity

42. It can be inferred that man's inventions may lead to his

  (A) Prosperity   (B) Slavery
  (C) Freedom   (D) Improvement
  (E) Comfort

43. The writer believes that the chief concern of society should be

  (A) The development of machinery for the betterment of life
  (B) The organization of labor unions
  (C) The control of competition in economic trading
  (D) The care and culture of its members
  (E) The establishment of a minimum wage

44. Judging from the passage, which of the following would the author be most likely to favor?

  (A) Free trade   (B) Increased productivity
  (C) Well-educated workers   (D) Specialized laborers
  (E) Food inspectors

45. Of the following, which inference about commerce does the passage best support?

  (A) That machines enhance man's potential
  (B) Competition reduces quality
  (C) Trade discourages deception
  (D) Work ennobles man
  (E) Pollution injures agriculture

Skill Builder—Reading Comprehension

Following each passage is a question or group of questions based on its content. Select the best answer to each question. The answers will be reviewed in televised Verbal Lesson One or by your classroom teacher.

Exercise A: Social Studies

Recently in the United States we have seen a proliferation of governmental regulations regarding the economy. Typically, these regulations have been reported in newspapers
5 under the all-encompassing phrase, "price controls." The prices of both goods and services are affected. The prices charged by public utilities such as gas and electric are fixed by the government. Rates charged by airlines
10 must receive the stamp of government ap-

8

proval. Certain industries such as steel and oil are granted tax allowances. The number of operating radio and television stations is controlled and their advertising rates are moni-
15 tored by a government agency.

1. The title that best expresses the passage is

   (A) Airline regulations
   (B) Tax allowances for American industries
   (C) Regulating public utilities
   (D) Governmental control of the economy
   (E) Price fixing

2. State in your own words the *main* idea of the passage.

   _____

   _____

   _____

Exercise B: Biological Science

The use of antibiotics in modern medicine has obviously been a boon to the health of the world's populace but the lessons learned in their application have been surprising and,
5 at times, costly. Antibiotics are bacteria-killing substances produced by living organisms. The accidental discovery of penicillin by Sir Alexander Fleming in 1929 helped combat infections but allergic reactions to this
10 drug were discovered to be amazingly common. In some cases, the reactions were strong enough to be fatal. Dr. Selman Waksman's discover of streptomycin, another antibiotic, was a major breakthrough in man's fight
15 against tuberculosis, whooping cough, and certain forms of pneumonia. However, if its usage is not strictly controlled certain strains of the bacteria, which it is intended to destroy, may resist and survive and, in
20 the end, a whole new strain of bacteria may develop in which all members resist the antibiotic. Thus the opposite result is achieved and the antibiotic becomes totally ineffectual.

3. Which of the following titles best describes the content of the passage?

   (A) The uses of antibiotics
   (B) Antibiotics as bacteria killers
   (N) Penicillin and streptomycin
   (D) The fight against disease
   (E) Perils in the use of antibiotics

Exercise C: Argumentative

A mere scholar, who knows nothing but books, must be ignorant even of them. Books do not teach the use of books. How should he know anything of a work who knows noth-
5 ing of the subject of it? The learned pedant is conversant with books only as they are made of other books. He parrots those who have parroted others. He can translate the same word into 10 different languages, but
10 he knows nothing of the thing which it means in any one of them. He stuffs his head with authorities built on authorities, with quotations quoted from quotations, while he locks up his senses, his understanding and his heart.
15 He is unacquainted with the maxims and manners of the world he is to seek in the characters of individuals. He sees no beauty in the face of nature or of art. To him the mighty world of eye and ear is hid; and knowl-
20 edge, except at one entrance, quite shut out. His pride takes par with his ignorance; and his self-importance rises with the number of things of which he does not know the value, and which he therefore despises as unworthy
25 of his notice.
(William Hazlitt, *On the Ignorance of the Learned*)

4. The primary point of the passage is that

(A) Knowledge is derived from a thorough study of the world's great books
(B) Books contain ideas that have already been written down in other books
(C) To be considered intelligent a scholar must be conversant with books
(D) True understanding requires both reading and experience
(E) Most scholars tend to become boastful and filled with pride

Exercise D: Narrative

A man can be asked once too often to act as chairman, and to such a man, despairing of his weakness and feeling a thousand miles from any delight, I can suggest a few devices.
5 In introducing one or two of the chief speakers, grossly over-praise them but put no warmth into your voice, only a metallic flavour of irony. If you know what a speaker's main point is to be, then make it neatly in
10 presenting him to the audience. During some tremendous peroration, which the chap has been working at for days, either begin whispering and passing notes to other speakers or give the appearance of falling asleep in
15 spite of much effort to keep awake. If the funny man takes possession of the meeting

and brings out the old jokes, either look
melancholy or raise your eyebrows as high as
they will go. Announce the fellow with the
20 weak delivery in your loudest and clearest
tones. For any timid speaker, officiously clear
a space bang in the middle and offer him
water, paper, pencil, a watch, anything.
(J. B. Priestley, *Quietly Malicious Chairman-
ship*)

Using your own words, write the most important point the writer makes in the above passage.

Now, answer the following questions.

5. Which of the following best summarizes the author's message?

    (A)   A successful chairman always praises the guest speaker
    (B)   The best chairmen are the loudest
    (C)   A successful chairman is quite noticeable
    (D)   To be elected chairman one must have considerable experience
    (E)   For those not wishing to remain chairman, a solution may be found

6. List at least three details that support the main idea.

    1. _____

    2. _____

    3. _____

7. The author's tone is

    (A)   Sincere
    (B)   Satiric
    (C)   Factual
    (D)   Bitter
    (E)   Respectful

Vocabulary Builder

Follow the instructions for each of the exercises. Answer keys are provided at the end of the vocabulary builder section. Before doing the exercises, familiarize *yourself with the* 20 Key Prefixes, 16 Important Roots, *and the* Essential Words.

20 Key Prefixes and 16 Important Roots

Prefixes	Roots
1. ad .... *to, toward* (Lat.)	1. cap(t) ..... *take, seize* (Lat.)
2. com .... *together, with* (Lat.)	2. cord .... *heart* (Lat.)
3. de.......... *away, down* (Lat.)	3. duc(t) ..... *lead* (Lat.)
4. dis.......... *apart, not* (Lat.)	4. fac(t)(fic). *make, do* (Lat.)

11

5. eu........... *well* (Gr.)
6. epi.......... *upon, over* (Gr.)
7. ex........... *out, beyond* (Lat.)
8. in........... *into, not* (Lat.)
9. inter....... *between, among* (Lat.)
10. mis......... *bad, wrong* (A. Sax.)
11. mono...... *alone, one* (Gr.)
12. non......... *not* (Lat.)
13. ob .... *against,* (also: *to, toward*) (Lat.)
14. over........ *above, beyond* (A. Sax.)
15. pre .... *before, beforehand* (Lat.)
16. pro .... *forward, for, before* (Lat.)
17. re .... *back, again* (Lat.)
18. sub......... *under, beneath* (Lat.)
19. trans....... *across, beyond, over, through* (Lat.)
20. un .... *not* (A. Sax.)

5. fer .... *bear, carry* (Lat.)
6. graph ...... *write* (Gr.)
7. log.......... *speech, word* (Gr.)
8. mit(t) ..... *send* (Lat.)
9. plic......... *fold* (Lat.)
10. pon......... *put, place* (Lat.)
11. scrib .... *write* (Lat.)
12. spec(t) .... *see* (Lat.)
13. sta.......... *stand* (Lat.)
14. tang........ *touch* (Lat.)
15. tend........ *stretch* (Lat.)
16. ten .... *hold, have* (Lat.)

Essential Words—Human Relations

1. Altruism—*(N)* concern for the welfare of others
2. Captious—*(Adj)* hard to please; faultfinding
3. Diffidence—*(N)* state of being diffident (lacking self-confidence, shy)
4. Facile—*(Adj)* easily done, used; taking little effort; working easily
5. Incredulous—*(Adj)* disbelieving, skeptical
6. Irascible—*(Adj)* easily angered, prone to outbursts of temper
7. Officious—*(Adj)* excessively forward in offering one's services or advice to others
8. Pariah—*(N)* any person or animal generally despised; outcast
9. Pedant—*(N)* one who pays undue attention to book learning; a doctrinaire
10. Perspicacity—*(N)* shrewdness; an ability to see through things
11. Pertinacious—*(Adj)* holding firmly to a purpose, action, or opinion; very persistent
12. Pragmatic—*(Adj)* concerned with practical results or values; viewing things in a matter-of-fact manner
13. Probity—*(N)* complete and confirmed integrity; uprightness, honesty
14. Suppliant—*(Adj)* asking humbly and earnestly; *(N)* a person who asks humbly and earnestly
15. Taciturn—*(Adj)* habitually untalkative; laconic; uncommunicative

Essential Words—World of Practical Affairs

1. Adulteration—*(N)* impure, corruption
2. Cohort—*(N)* one of the 10 divisions of a Roman legion; companion
3. Conscription—*(N)* compulsory service of men in the armed forces; draft; act of forcing contributions as the government directs
4. Deduction—*(N)* subtraction; reasoning from the general to the specific
5. Empirical—*(Adj)* based on experiment and observation
6. Exposition—*(N)* a public show; a detailed explanation; speech or writing explaining a process, thing, or idea

7. Hegemony—*(N)* political domination of one state over others in a group; leadership
8. Imperialism—*(N)* supreme authority, sovereign; system of an imperial government
9. Insurgency—*(N)* rising in nonbelligerent revolt against a government in power
10. Monograph—*(N)* a scholarly book, article, or pamphlet on a specific and limited subject
11. Monopoly—*(N)* the exclusive control of a commodity or service
12. Pacification—*(N)* placation; appeasement; peaceful submission
13. Peroration—*(N)* conclusion of a speech with a formal recapitulation
14. Subjugate—*(V)* to bring under dominion; conquer; subdue
15. Temperance—*(N)* moderation; self-restraint; abstinence from alcoholic liquors

Essential Words—Aesthetic–Philosophical

1. Circumspect—*(Adj)* watchful on all sides; cautious, careful
2. Contingent—*(N)* group of soldiers, laborers given to another; *(Adj)* conditional; liable to happen; possible
3. Countenance—*(N)* aspect, appearance
4. Efficacy—*(N)* power to produce the effect wanted; effectiveness
5. Extant—*(Adj)* still existing, not destroyed or lost
6. Intangible—*(Adj)* not capable of being touched or felt; not easily grasped by the mind
7 Maxim—*(N)* a succinct formulation of some fundamental principle or rule of conduct
8. Mitigate—*(V)* to moderate (a quality or condition) in force or intensity; alleviate
9. Ostensible—*(Adj)* given or appearing as such; seeming; professed
10. Ostentation—*(N)* a showing off; a display to impress others
11. Par—*(N)* an equal level; equality; average or normal amount
12. Proliferate—*(V)* grow or produce by multiplication of parts
13. Specious—*(Adj)* seeming desirable, reasonable, but not really so
14. Tantamount—*(Adj)* equivalent in effect or value; used with "to"
15. Tenet—*(N)* doctrine, principle, belief, or opinion held as true

Essential Words—Science Related

1. Circumscribe—*(V)* encircle, limit, restrict
2. Coniferous—*(Adj)* bearing cones
3. Deciduous—*(Adj)* shedding leaves annually; falling off at a particular stage of growth
4. Emit—*(V)* give off; send out; discharge
5. Facade—*(N)* front part of a building; any side of a building facing a street
6. Inert—*(Adj)* having no power to move or act; lifeless; sluggish; inactive
7. Juxtapose—*(V)* put close together; place side by side
8. Phylum—*(N)* a primary group of the animal or vegetable kingdom, ranking above a class
9. Specter—*(N)* ghost, phantom (terrifying in appearance)
10. Stamen—*(N)* part of a flower containing the pollen; threadlike stem that supports the anther
11. Static—*(Adj)* in a fixed or stable condition; at rest; standing still
12. Tactile—*(Adj)* having to do with touch; tangible
13. Tangent—*(Adj)* in contact; touching; (in geometry) touching a curve or surface at one point but not intersecting
14. Tenon—*(N)* projection on the end of a piece of wood cut so as to fit on to another to form a joint
15. Undulating—*(Adj-V)* moving in a smooth wavelike motion

Exercise I—Roots

Match the Root in Column A with its meaning in Column B.

Column A		Column B	
1.	cap(t)	(A)	make, do
2.	cord	(B)	write
3.	duc(t)	(C)	take, seize
4.	fac(t)(fic)	(D)	send
5.	fer	(E)	stand
6.	log	(F)	see
7.	mit(t)	(G)	stretch
8.	plic	(H)	heart
9.	pon	(I)	touch
10.	scrib-graph	(J)	bear, carry
11.	spec(t)	(K)	hold, have
12.	sta	(L)	lead
13.	tang	(M)	put, place
14.	ten	(N)	speech, word
15.	tend	(O)	fold

1. _____ 6. _____ 11. _____

2. _____ 7. _____ 12. _____

3. _____ 8. _____ 13. _____

4. _____ 9. _____ 14. _____

5. _____ 10. _____ 15. _____

Exercise 2—Prefixes

Match the Prefix in Column A with its meaning in Column B.

Column A		Column B	
1.	ad	(A)	between, among
2.	de	(B)	back, again
3.	dis	(C)	across, beyond
4.	epi	(D)	bad, wrong
5.	ex	(E)	apart, not
6.	in	(F)	not
7.	inter	(G)	out, beyond
8.	mis	(H)	to, toward
9.	ob	(I)	into, not
10.	over	(J)	away, down
11.	pro	(K)	above, beyond
12.	re	(L)	forward, for
13.	trans	(M)	upon, over
14.	un	(N)	against (also to, toward)

1. _____ 8. _____

2. _____ 9. _____

3. _____ 10. _____

4. _____ 11. _____

5. _____   12. _____

6. _____   13. _____

7. _____   14. _____

Exercise 3

For each of the key words in Exercise 3 select from the list below one word that is most nearly the same in meaning to the key word and one word that is most nearly opposite to the key word. The first one is done for you.

<u>Synonyms</u>

1. advocate
2. argument
3. aromatic
4. artificial
5. cohesive
6. commend
7. criminal
8. drowsy
9. duplicate
10. elicit
11. expand
12. faultfinding
13. flexible
14. forbid
15. hidden
16. illogical
17. innovation
18. involve
19. malign
20. one-sided
21. persuade
22. real
23. sincere
24. spacious
25. tractable

<u>Antonyms</u>

acceptable
alert
antagonist
approving
archaic
authorize
benefactor
brittle
compatibility
condemn
deter
extricate
feigned
genuine
incomprehensible
intractable
irresolute
limited
original
praise
prominent
repress
scentless
shrink
unbiased

<u>1. Capacious</u>
KEY WORD

| _____ | <u>cap(ac)</u> | <u>(i)ous</u> |
| prefix(es) | root | suffix(es) |

| <u>able to contain much</u> | <u>capable of holding a large quantity; roomy</u> |
| literal meaning | definition |

| <u>spacious</u> | <u>limited</u> |
| synonym | antonym |

15

2. Captious
KEY WORD

prefix(es)	capt	(i)ous
	root	suffix(es)

ensnaring; seizure	intended to confuse or to entrap in argument
literal meaning	definition

synonym	antonym

3. Contention
KEY WORD

con	ten(d)	tion
prefix(es)	root	suffix(es)

the act of stretching together	verbal argument; quarrel; a point affirmed in controversy; contest
literal meaning	definition

synonym	antonym

4. Cordial
KEY WORD

prefix(es)	cord	ial
	root	suffix(es)

belonging to the heart	genuinely warm and friendly; hearty (full of affection)
literal meaning	definition

synonym	antonym

5. Distend
KEY WORD

dis	ten(d)	
prefix(es)	root	suffix(es)

to stretch apart	spreading in all directions; to enlarge by pressure from within
literal meaning	definition

expand	shrink
synonym	antonym

6. Ductile
KEY WORD

	duct	ile
prefix(es)	root	suffix(es)

pertaining to the ability to lead (shape)	capable of being shaped; molded
literal meaning	definition

synonym	antonym

7. Eulogize
KEY WORD

eu	log	ize
prefix(es)	root	suffix(es)

to speak well of	to praise highly in speech or writing
literal meaning	definition

synonym	antonym

8. Evoke
KEY WORD

e	voke	
prefix(es)	root	suffix(es)

to call out	to call forth
literal meaning	definition

synonym	antonym

9. Facsimile
KEY WORD

	fac/simile	
prefix(es)	root	suffix(es)

make similar	exact copy or reproduction
literal meaning	definition

synonym	antonym

10. Factitious
KEY WORD

prefix(es)	fact	(it)ious
	root	suffix(es)

made by art	lacking authenticity; produced artificially
literal meaning	definition

synonym	antonym

11. Implicate
KEY WORD

im	plic	ate
prefix(es)	root	suffix(es)

to fold in	to have a part in; to connect with
literal meaning	definition

synonym	antonym

12. Induce
KEY WORD

in	duce	
prefix(es)	root	suffix(es)

to lead in; motivate	to cause; to prevail upon; to bring about
literal meaning	definition

synonym	antonym

13. Interdict
KEY WORD

inter	dict	
prefix(es)	root	suffix(es)

to speak between	to prohibit; forbid
literal meaning	definition

forbid	
synonym	antonym

14. Malefactor
KEY WORD

male/fact	or
root	suffix(es)

_____ prefix(es)

one who does bad; evildoer	one who commits a crime
literal meaning	definition

synonym	antonym

15. Neologism
KEY WORD

neo	log	ism
prefix(es)	root	suffix(es)

pertaining to a new word	a new word or use of word
literal meaning	definition

synonym	antonym

16. Odoriferous
KEY WORD

odor/i/fer	ous
root	suffix(es)

_____ prefix(es)

to bring odor	having an odor, especially a pleasant one
literal meaning	definition

synonym	antonym

17. Pliable
KEY WORD

pli	able
root	suffix(es)

_____ prefix(es)

able to bend or fold	easily bent; readily yielding to force or pressure
literal meaning	definition

synonym	antonym

19

18. Proponent
KEY WORD

pro	pon	ent
prefix(es)	root	suffix(es)

a person who places before (sets forth)	a person who puts forward a proposal
literal meaning	definition

synonym	antonym

19. Soporific
KEY WORD

	sopor/fic	
prefix(es)	root	suffix(es)

bringing sleep	tending to cause sleep
literal meaning	definition

synonym	antonym

20. Tangible
KEY WORD

	tang	ible
prefix(es)	root	suffix(es)

can be touched	capable of being touched; definite
literal meaning	definition

synonym	antonym

21. Tenacious
KEY WORD

	tenaci	ous
prefix(es)	root	suffix(es)

full of holding (fast)	holding fast, highly retentive
literal meaning	definition

synonym	antonym

22. Tendentious
KEY WORD

	tendenti	ous
prefix(es)	root	suffix(es)

to extend in a definite way	having a definite tendency; advancing a definite point of view
literal meaning	definition

synonym	antonym

23. Traduce
KEY WORD

tra	duce	
prefix(es)	root	suffix(es)

to lead across (dishonor)	to speak falsely of; to slander
literal meaning	definition

synonym	antonym

24. Inconspicuous
KEY WORD

in/con	spic	uous
prefix(es)	root	suffix(es)

not visible	not easily seen; not worthy of notice; likely to escape notice
literal meaning	definition

synonym	antonym

25. Untenable
KEY WORD

un	ten	able
prefix(es)	root	suffix(es)

not capable of being held	not able to be defended
literal meaning	definition

synonym	antonym

Exercise 4—Root Words and Meanings

Fill in the blanks with the correct words.

1. The root _____ is found in *captious.*

    CAPTIOUS means _____ .

2. The root _____ is found in *cordial.*

    CORDIAL means _____ .

3. The root _____ is found in *deduction.*

    DEDUCTION means _____ .

4. The root _____ is found in *explicit.*

    EXPLICIT means _____ .

5. The root _____ is found in *extend.*

    EXTEND means _____ .

6. The root _____ is found in *factor.*

    FACTOR means _____ .

7. The root _____ is found in *logistics.*

    LOGISTICS means _____ .

8. The root _____ is found in *prescribe.*

    PRESCRIBE means _____ .

9. The root _____ is found in *tangible.*

    TANGIBLE means _____ .

10. The root _____ is found in *tenacious.*

    TENACIOUS means _____ .

Exercise 5—Essential Words

Match each word in Column A with its definition in Column B.

Column A

1. adulterate I
2. altruistic E
3. circumscribe J
4. incredulous C
5. mitigate D
6. officious B
7. pacify F
8. probity A
9. specious G
10. subjugate H

Column B

(A) complete honesty
(B) excessively forward in offering one's services
(C) unbelieving
(D) alleviate
(E) motivated by unselfishness
(F) restore to tranquility
(G) seemingly true but actually false
(H) conquer
(I) make impure
(J) to set the limits of

1. _____   6. _____

2. _____   7. _____

3. _____   8. _____

4. _____   9. _____

5. _____   10. _____

Exercise 6—Antonyms

Match each word in Column A with the word most nearly opposite in Column B.

<u>Column A</u>

1. admit
2. adulteration
3. altruism
4. diffident
5. discord
6. distend
7. explicit
8. monologs
9. probity
10. taciturn

<u>Column B</u>

(A) talkative
(B) confident
(C) dishonesty
(D) debates
(E) obscure
(F) unison
(G) pureness
(H) selfishness
(I) bar
(J) shrink

1. _I_____   6. _J_____

2. _G_____   7. _E_____

3. _H_____   8. _D_____

4. _B_____   9. _C_____

5. _F_____   10. _A_____

Exercise 7—Sentence Completion

Complete the sentences in Column B by filling in the blank with the correct word from Column A. Some words will be used more than once.

<u>Column A</u>

1. contention
2. countenance
3. distended
4. explicit
5. implicate
6. irascible

<u>Column B</u>

1. He gave ___4___ directions.

2. Many criminals often ___5___ others.

3. A table is a ___9___ object.

4. Because he was so ___6___, others avoided him.

5. He had a ___10___ grip on my arm.

6. The material that was used was very ___8___.

23

7. ostensible
8. pliable
9. tangible
10. tenacious

7. They had no ___9___ evidence to prove his guilt.

8. As air filled the balloon it ___3___ almost to the point of bursting.

9. To prove your innocence, you must be more ___4___.

10. Forgetting nothing, he had a ___10___ memory.

11. He is too ___6___ to be the leader of the group.

12. Isaac Newton's ___11___ about gravity proved to be valid.

13. By his ___2___ you could tell that he was the leader of the group.

14. His ___7___ purpose was charity; his real purpose was popularity.

Vocabulary Check Test

(Answers will be reviewed in televised Verbal Lesson One or by your classroom teacher.)

Part A

Choose the word or phrase most nearly opposite to the word in capital letters.

1. DIFFIDENCE:
   (A) impropriety   (B) eminence   (C) observance
   (D) confidence   (E) secretiveness

2. PERORATE:
   (A) speak harshly   (B) give orders   (C) grant permission
   (D) seek advice   (E) say a few words

3. INDUCE:
   (A) exhaust   (B) impel   (C) jeopardize
   (D) hamper   (E) acquaint

4. SPECULATE:
   (A) spell out   (B) celebrate   (C) verify
   (D) besmirch   (E) ponder

5. IMPLICATE:
   (A) escape   (B) exonerate   (C) premeditate
   (D) delude   (E) require

6. PROBITY:
   (A) loyalty   (B) dishonesty   (C) likelihood
   (D) painfulness   (E) excitability

7. INCREDULOUS:
   (A) unfeeling   (B) sensitive   (C) durable
   (D) gullible   (E) faultless

8. OSTENSIBLE:
   (A) ceremonial   (B) skeptical   (C) genuine
   (D) conspicuous   (E) restrictive

9. MITIGATE:
   (A) harmonize   (B) misjudge   (C) idle
   (D) engulf   (E) aggravate

10. CAPACIOUS:
    (A) limited   (B) charming   (C) ample
    (D) captured   (E) easily managed

11. MALEFACTION:
    (A) cowardice   (B) deception   (C) bane
    (D) curiosity   (E) good deed

24

12. TACITURN:　　　　　(A) chivalrous　　　(B) loquacious　　　(C) obtuse
　　　　　　　　　　　(D) grim　　　　　　(E) detailed

13. CONSPICUOUS:　　　(A) infamous　　　　(B) indiscrete　　　(C) unimportant
　　　　　　　　　　　(D) accidental　　　(E) occasional

14. DUCTILE:　　　　　(A) landless　　　　(B) brittle　　　　(C) filtered
　　　　　　　　　　　(D) automatic　　　(E) luscious

15. EVOKE:　　　　　　(A) prevent　　　　(B) erase　　　　(C) unravel
　　　　　　　　　　　(D) expose　　　　(E) welcome

Part B

From the list below choose the word that best completes the analogy by expressing a relationship similar to that expressed in the original pair.

(A) proponent　　　　　　　　　(F) interdiction
(B) imperialism　　　　　　　　(G) conduit
(C) sagacity　　　　　　　　　(H) odoriferousness
(D) neologism　　　　　　　　(I) altruism
(E) tenacity　　　　　　　　　(J) legislators

16. Protector: defender:: advocate: _A_____

17. Denial: refusal:: taboo: _F_____

18. Forsooth: archaism:: bikini: _D_____

19. Lamp: light:: glue: _G_____

20. Radio: transmitter:: water: _G_____

21. Fog: dampness:: rose: _H_____

22. Hoarding: selfishness:: charity: _I_____

23. Salesman: customers:: lobbyist: _J_____

24. Pollution: harmful environment:: conquest: _B_____

25. Irascibility: serenity:: senility: _C_____

Part C

From the list below select the words that best fit the meaning or context of the sentence.

(1) altruistic　　　　　　　　(6) inimical
(2) circumscribe　　　　　　　(7) irascible
(3) contentious　　　　　　　(8) officious
(4) factitious　　　　　　　　(9) sagacious
(5) incredulous　　　　　　　(10) soporific

26. Those who behave in an _____ manner can never be _____ or wise; their emotions

　　chain their minds.

25

27. In one sense technology may be viewed as a means for man to _____ his _____ environment.

28. In spite of high fences an _____ or meddlesome attitude often leads to _____ neighbors.

29. One questions the _____ motives of those volunteers who present a _____ request for donations.

30. An _____ reader finds it difficult to believe that the liquor in the keg from which Rip Van Winkle drank could have had such a _____ effect.

Verbal
Lesson
Two

Simulated Verbal Examination

Time—30 Minutes

(The answers to the examination will be reviewed in televised Verbal Lesson Two or by your classroom teacher.)

Segment 1: Opposites

Select the word that is most nearly opposite in meaning to the word or phrase in capital letters. Consider any fine shades of meaning that may exist.

Example:

HOT: (A) green   (B) river   (C) cold
         (D) above   (E) sweet

	A	B	C	D	E
	○	○	●	○	○

1. LAMENT: (A) encroach   (B) excuse   (C) rejoice
                  (D) repair   (E) adhere

2. EXPLICIT: (A) loud   (B) erring   (C) provisional
                  (D) ambiguous (E) evil

3. LUDICROUS: (A) amiable   (B) luminous   (C) transparent
                  (D) criminal   (E) serious

4. TUMULTUOUS: (A) gigantic   (B) prosperous (C) infinitesimal
                  (D) orderly   (E) impetuous

5. LUXURIANT: (A) sparse   (B) posh   (C) prominent
                  (D) torrid   (E) wealthy

6. PROFLIGATE: (A) decorative (B) profound   (C) talkative
                  (D) profitable (E) virtuous

7. LASCIVIOUS: (A) chaste   (B) sympathetic (C) devious
                  (D) contagious (E) controversial

8. EMBOLDEN: (A) etch   (B) discourage (C) embellish
                  (D) deface   (E) symbolize

9. REFRACTORY: (A) reflective (B) shadowy   (C) transient
                  (D) flimsy   (E) malleable

10. BIZARRE: (A) marketable (B) suave   (C) conventional
                  (D) famous   (E) controversial

27

Segment 2: Sentence Completion

The blanks in each sentence indicate omitted words. Select the word or words that best fit the meaning of the entire sentence and should be inserted in the blank.

Example:

On a small farm in an arid climate one should not grow crops that need considerable _____

or _____ to ripen.

(A) fertilizer — attention   (B) space — water
(C) sun — air   (D) tilling — harvesting
(E) weeding — insecticides

A B C D E
○ ● ○ ○ ○

11. In spite of an increased military commitment by the enemy, the Prime Minister continued his efforts to prevent _____ _____ of the war.

    (A) a deterioration   (B) an intensification
    (C) a restoration   (D) a renunciation
    (E) a prolongation

12. Blessings on him who invented _____, the mantle that covers all human thoughts, the food that appeases hunger, the general _____ that purchases all things.

    (A) darkness — fund   (B) silence — wealth
    (C) imagination — syndicate   (D) sleep — coin
    (E) doubt — skeptic

13. Recognition of the falsity of _____ wealth as the standard of success goes hand in hand with the _____ of the false belief that high political positions are to be valued only by the standards of personal profit.

    (A) financial — retention   (B) material — abandonment
    (C) national — concurrence   (D) intangible — rejection
    (E) individual — abhorrence

14. The behavior of the insane is merely _____ behavior, a bit more exaggerated and distorted.

    (A) sane   (B) moribund
    (C) odious   (D) idiosyncratic
    (E) reticent

15. The need for television viewing guides is _____ by a study that shows that viewers tend not to select programs by _____ switching the dial.

    (A) questioned — quickly   (B) lessened — carefully
    (C) supported — randomly   (D) confirmed — frequently
    (E) strengthened — skillfully

Segment 3: Analogies

Each question below contains a related pair of words or phrases followed by five lettered pairs of words or phrases. Select the answer that best expresses a relationship similar to that expressed in the original pair.

28

Example:

PURSUE: CATCH::

(A) occur: happen
(C) track: overtake
(E) contest: victory

(B) eat: drink
(D) apprehend: chase

```
A   B   C   D   E
○   ○   ●   ○   ○
```

16. GALE: HURRICANE::

    (A) cyclone: squall
    (C) breeze: draft
    (E) doldrums: cloudburst

    (B) overshadow: eclipse
    (D) snowstorm: blizzard

17. EARTH: SOLAR SYSTEM::

    (A) planet: sun
    (C) universe: galaxy
    (E) land: continent

    (B) moon: rings
    (D) tree: forest

18. ARTIFICIAL: NATURAL::

    (A) warrior: champion
    (C) ideal: prototype
    (E) eternal: finite

    (B) copied: substitute
    (D) lithograph: oil painting

19. ATOLL: CORAL::

    (A) farm: vegetables
    (C) region: surface
    (E) horseshoe: blacksmith

    (B) volcano: lava
    (D) island: water

20. BALANCE: ACROBATICS::

    (A) radar: bats
    (C) dexterity: surgery
    (E) pencil: writing

    (B) voice: pitch
    (D) stamina: success

21. FRUSTRATION: RAGE::

    (A) unhappiness: despair
    (C) despondency: depression
    (E) endurance: fatigue

    (B) injustice: anger
    (D) caring: loathing

22. ECUMENICAL: UNIVERSAL::

    (A) isthmus: land
    (C) harmony: music
    (E) monopoly: competition

    (B) infringement: violation
    (D) soliloquy: listener

23. PLEASURE: ECSTASY::

    (A) despair: cheerfulness
    (C) happiness: bliss
    (E) gratification: enjoyment

    (B) euphoria: exaltation
    (D) rapture: delight

24. CODICIL: WILL::

    (A) chapter: volume
    (C) contract: marriage
    (E) descendant: inheritance

    (B) introduction: presentation
    (D) sequel: literary work

25. APHORISM: ABSURDITY::

    (A) sacred: worship   (B) proverb: adage
    (C) truth: fidelity   (D) capitulation: conquest
    (E) virtue: conformity

Segment 4: Reading Comprehension

The questions following each passage are based on its content. Your choice should be made on the basis of what is stated *or implied in the passage.*

In view of the part that the commander of the *Indomitable* plays in scenes shortly to follow, it may be well to fill out that sketch of him outlined in the previous chapter.

5   Aside from his qualities as a sea officer Captain Vere was an exceptional character. Unlike no few of England's renowned sailors, long and arduous service, with signal devotion to it, had not resulted in absorbing and salting
10   the entire man. He had a marked leaning toward everything intellectual. He loved books, never going to sea without a newly replenished library, compact but of the best. The isolated leisure, in some cases so weari-
15   some, falling at intervals to commanders even during a war cruise, never was tedious to Captain Vere. His bias was toward those books to which every serious mind of superior order occupying any active post of authority
20   in the world naturally inclines: books treating of actual men and events no matter of what era—history, biography, and unconventional writers, who, free from cant and convention, like Montaigne, honestly and in the spirit of
25   common sense philosophize upon realities.

In this love of reading he found confirmation of his own more reasoned thoughts— confirmation which he had vainly sought in social converse—so that, as touching most
30   fundamental topics, there had got to be established in him some positive convictions, which he forefelt would abide in him essentially unmodified so long as his intelligent part remained unimpaired. In view of the
35   troubled period in which his lot was cast this was well for him. His settled convictions were as a dike against those invading waters of novel opinion, social, political, and otherwise, which carried away as in a torrent no few
40   minds in those days, minds by nature not inferior to his own. While other members of that aristocracy to which by birth he belonged were incensed at the innovators mainly because their theories were inimical to the

30

⁴⁵ privileged classes, not alone Captain Vere
disinterestedly opposed them because they
seemed to him incapable of embodiment in
lasting institutions, but at war with the peace
of the world and the true welfare of mankind.
(Herman Melville, *Billy Budd*)

26. Which *best* characterizes Captain Vere's love of books?

    I. His library contained a small but sufficiently wide variety of the best books

    II. He preferred non-fiction books

    III. He preferred books that reinforced his own convictions

    IV. He opposed new ideas hostile to the privileged class

    (A) I and II only   (B) II and III only
    (C) II and IV only   (D) I and III only
    (E) I and IV only

27. In his description of Captain Vere the author makes use of all of the following <u>except</u>

    (A) Contrast   (B) Analogy
    (C) Satire   (D) Figurative language
    (E) Foreshadowing

28. The author describes Captain Vere as exceptional because unlike most officers in the naval service

    (A) His devotion to duty remained constant
    (B) He failed to demonstrate an excessive love of glory
    (C) His character had not deteriorated after so long a service
    (D) He was an aristocrat
    (E) He had only served during peacetime

29. According to the author, Captain Vere considered his leisure time at sea

    (A) To be tedious
    (B) An opportunity to solve his crew's problems
    (C) An opportunity to write about his exploits
    (D) An opportunity to relax
    (E) An opportunity to read

30. Based on the information in the passage it can be inferred that

    (A) Captain Vere was a liberal thinker
    (B) Captain Vere was an ineffective leader
    (C) Captain Vere was a brilliant naval tactician
    (D) Captain Vere preferred the intellectual stimulation of books to other men's conversation
    (E) Captain Vere shunned the aristocracy

The twentieth century has witnessed an increased interest and excitement in John Donne's *Songs and Sonnets*. Some of the reasons why Donne's lyrics appeal so much ⁵ to modern taste are his somewhat unconventional attitudes towards love, his anti-establishment poses, and his highly dramatic presentation of the love relationship. The Renaissance was a period in history when the

31

traditional standards of morality were beginning to be questioned; a time when the advent of science and its accompanying techniques brought all fields of knowledge into question; a time of exploration and experimentation. Donne exhibits the vitality and excitement of the Renaissance in the *Songs and Sonnets* and the twentieth century reader, living in a somewhat similar period, feels a rapport with Donne's attitudes.

Donne breaks with the tradition of Petrarchan lyricism and poses realistic love affairs with all their sensuous qualities in his lyrics. He replaces the "tear floods" and "sigh tempests" of Petrarchism* with dialectical arguments professing promiscuity. The language he uses bears few resemblances to the MELLIFLUOUS strains of the Elizabethan lyric. In fact, one of the constant criticisms of Donne is that he has a relatively dull ear to the sonorities of language. Despite the lack of musical qualities in his language, Donne's highly dramatic style and use of the dramatic monologue always make him an exciting writer. The use of the extended metaphor or "conceit" in his poems has enabled the poets who followed him to use the total range of language.

However, Donne's image as tradition-breaker, as iconoclast, has perhaps been overemphasized. Although it is indisputable that Donne had presented the antithesis to the contemporary standards of morality, it is perhaps time to counterbalance this view of Donne by examining his work in light of the preceding literary traditions. Although he breaks with much of the Petrarchan tradition concerning the love relationship, it is interesting to note that he borrows heavily from the same tradition for his own purposes. To see him merely as an innovator is to ignore the tremendous influence of the same tradition that he so devilishly enjoys spoofing.

*Petrarchism refers to poetry that is notable for its formal style, grammatical complexity, and elaborate, figurative language.

31. Which of the following best describes the passage?
   (A) John Donne's *Songs and Sonnets*
   (B) John Donne: Innovator and Traditionalist
   (C) John Donne and the Literary Tradition
   (D) John Donne: Immoralist
   (E) John Donne: Iconoclast

32. Which of the following statements is most compatible with the author's beliefs?

    (A) The language Donne uses in his poetry is filled with colorless imagery
    (B) To characterize Donne simply as an innovator is to make a very complex poet simple
    (C) Donne introduced a formal, complex vocabulary to his poetry
    (D) Donne's renewed popularity among modern readers is a result of the public's distaste for unconventional attitudes toward love
    (E) Donne's poetry reflects the style and content of the earlier Elizabethan poetry

33. MELLIFLUOUS on line 27 means

    (A) Ungrammatical
    (B) Inventive
    (C) Pleasant sounding
    (D) Harsh
    (E) Jovial

34. The function of the third (or last) paragraph is to

    (A) Give examples of Donne's break with tradition
    (B) Reverse previously expressed thoughts concerning Donne's characteristics
    (C) Substantiate that Donne follows the Petrarchan tradition
    (D) Document how Donne appeals to modern tastes
    (E) Urge the public not to read Donne's poetry

35. According to the passage, modern readers have shown a renewed interest in Donne's poetry because

      I. He expresses anti-establishment attitudes
     II. He demonstrates a dramatic writing style
    III. He exhibits the vitality of the Renaissance

    (A) I only   (B) II only
    (C) III only   (D) I and II only
    (E) I, II, and III

Our alphabet, a writing system based on the principle of one symbol, or letter, for each peculiar sound of language, is mankind's most convenient and most common system of

5   writing. Very few languages do not utilize an alphabet. Today there are over 50 different alphabetical systems in use, varying significantly in form, historical development, and in the extent to which one letter represents one

10 sound. However, the Chinese and Japanese do not use an alphabet. No sinologist can know all the 80,000 or so Chinese symbols and very few can master the approximately 9,000 symbols actually applied by Chinese

15 scholars. How much simpler it is to use 20, 23, or 26 signs.

Strange that such a powerful way of recording language was so long in coming. Considering the crucial role it plays today, it is

20 ironic that man has been writing for less than 6,000 years, a very short period of human history. He has been using the alphabet for

less than 4,000 years. Necessity and circumstance altered the ancient Semitic symbol aleph, meaning ox, into alpha, the first letter of the Greek alphabet and forerunner of our A. The symbol itself consisted of a line with two branching intersecting lines graphically representing the head and the extending horns of an ox. Similarly, our letter B evolved from beth, meaning house, which became the Greek beta. Sometime after 1,000 B.C. when the Etruscans moved into Central Italy from the eastern Mediterranean region, they carried with them the Greek alphabet and gave it much the same form we use today. The early Roman alphabet contained about 20 letters, eventually gaining 3 more.

Thanks to the simplicity of the alphabet, writing has become very common, its primary purposes being to communicate ideas and to record mankind's increasingly complex civilization. It is through writing that we preserve and transmit knowledge about our elaborate technologies, economies, literature, law, and other specializations. No longer is writing the exclusive domain of the priestly or other privileged classes as it was in Egypt or Mesopotamia. Elementary education begins with reading and writing. The printing press, the typewriter, shorthand, and the computer have had little impact upon alphabetic writing, which has survived with relatively little change for four millennia. Our writing is limited only by what we have to say and our capacity for knowledge, not by our alphabet.

36. According to the author, which of the following is (are) true of **alphabetical writing systems**?

   I. They are characterized by simplicity
   II. They are characterized by adaptability
   III. They are characterized by impracticability

   (A) I only
   (C) I and II only
   (E) I, II, and III

   (B) II only
   (D) II and III only

37. The writer states that the roots of our modern alphabet may be traced to

   (A) The Egyptians
   (C) The Chinese
   (E) The Germans

   (B) The Phoenicians
   (D) Ancient Semitic tribes

38. The word alphabet comes from the

   (A) Latin
   (C) Greek
   (E) Italian

   (B) Etruscan
   (D) Mesopotamian

39. Judging from the passage, the fact that alphabetic writing has survived with relatively little change indicates

    (A) Its suitability to serve the needs of a modern world
    (B) Its inadequacy in a rapidly changing world
    (C) That language has not been susceptible to change
    (D) The rigidity of spelling patterns
    (E) That most languages are derived from the same alphabet

40. It can be inferred from the passage that

    (A) Writing ensures the permanence of a language
    (B) English is a strictly phonetic writing system
    (C) All civilized cultures utilize an alphabetical form of writing
    (D) There are 26 sounds in the English language
    (E) The alphabet must bear some agreed upon relationship to the spoken form of a language

Skill Builder—Reading Comprehension

Following each passage is a question or group of questions based on its content. Select the best answer to each question. The answers will be reviewed in televised Verbal Lesson Two or by your classroom teacher.

Exercise A: Scientific

Imagine that we stand on an ordinary seaside pier, and watch the waves rolling in and striking against the iron columns of the pier. Large waves pay very little attention to the columns—they divide right and left and reunite after passing each column, much as a regiment of soldiers would if a tree stood in their road; it is almost as though the columns had not been there. But the short waves and ripples find the columns of the pier a much more formidable obstacle. When the short waves impinge on the columns, they are reflected back and spread as new ripples in all directions. To use the technical term, they are "scattered." The obstacle provided by the iron columns hardly affects the long waves at all, but scatters the short ripples.

We have been watching a sort of working model of the way in which sunlight struggles through the earth's atmosphere. Between us on earth and outer space the atmosphere interposes innumerable obstacles in the form of molecules of air, tiny droplets of water, and small particles of dust. These are represented by the columns of the pier.

The waves of the sea represent the sunlight. We know that sunlight is a blend of many colors—as we can prove for ourselves by passing it through a prism, or even through a

30 jug of water, or as nature demonstrates to us when she passes it through the raindrops of a summer shower and produces a rainbow. We also know that light consists of waves, and that the different colors of light are produced

35 by waves of different lengths, red light by long waves and blue light by short waves. The mixture of waves that constitutes sunlight has to struggle past the columns of the pier. And these obstacles treat the light-waves

40 much as the columns of the pier treat the sea-waves. The long waves that constitute red light are hardly affected but the short waves that constitute blue light are scattered in all directions.

45 Thus the different constituents of sunlight are treated in different ways as they struggle. through the earth's atmosphere. A wave of blue light may be scattered by a dust particle, and turned out of its course. After a time a

50 second dust particle again turns it out of its course, and so on, until finally it enters our eyes by a path as zigzag as that of a flash of lightning. Consequently the blue waves of the sunlight enter our eyes from all directions.

55 And that is why the sky looks blue.
(Sir James Jeans, *Why the Sky Is Blue*)

1. The sky is most likely to have a reddish glow at dawn because

    (A) The air temperature is usually higher at noon than at other times of the day
    (B) The ultraviolet rays of sunlight are chiefly responsible for the reddish glow
    (C) The earth's surface is slightly closer to the sun at noon than at dawn or dusk
    (D) The noonday sun is capable of producing more long waves than the morning or afternoon sun
    (E) The sun's angle is lower in the sky at dusk and at dawn causing the longer red rays to pass through a more absorbing atmosphere

2. The writer develops his topic mainly by means of

    (A) Sarcasm
    (B) Parody
    (C) Analogy
    (D) Figurative language
    (E) Allegory

Exercise B: Social Studies

Originally man appears to have been a polygamous animal. The foundations of the Judaic-Christian heritage, however, are ostensibly monogamous. The Catholic and

5 Greek Churches make marriage a sacrament, and many other creeds hold that the presence

of an officiating clergyman, if not actually obligatory, is "correct." Although modern-day marriages are based on the ideals of love, beauty, and free choice, many of the social customs that surround these ceremonies have their roots in a pagan past that emphasized the servitude and subjugation of women.

In the past marriage was first intertribal, and then EXOGAMOUS. The first form of exogamous marriage was marriage by capture. The bridegroom simply went out on the warpath, accompanied by a friend or two, seized upon such damsel as had strayed away from parental covert, and carried her away to his home. In our modern marriage rite the very name of that now useless appendage the "best man" suggests that he is a relic of marriage by capture. He was the strong armed warrior who assisted the would-be groom to carry off his bride. The wedding ring symbolizes the fetter with which the bride was bound. The honeymoon itself symbolizes that space of time when the captor had to hide his prize from her kinsmen until their consent had been gained.

Marriage by purchase succeeded marriage by capture. Indeed, the two gradually merged together in the latter days of the capture period. The pursuing father gradually learned to mitigate his wrath in the presence of cash or other equivalent. This kind of marriage is still prevalent among developing nations. The bridegroom might offer in lieu of cash his own sister, or horses, or cattle, or land. Perhaps the most perfect system of marriage by purchase was that of the Babylonian and Assyrians. They assembled all girls of marriageable age in the space before the temple twice a year, and sold them. The handsome girls brought high prices, and the sums so received were turned over to the homely ones as a counterattraction. Thus every girl caught a husband.

Ritualistic marriage ceremonies, some of which continued into the Twentieth Century, signified female subjugation. In Australia a woman carried fire to her lover's hut and made a fire for him. In Angola she cooked two dishes for him in his shelter. In Croatia the bridegroom boxed the bride's ears, and in some parts of Russia the father formerly struck his daughter gently with a new whip—for the last time—and then gave the weapon to her husband. In the Zulu ceremony the

37

bride was formally told that she must submit
to domination by her mother-in-law,
and to brutality from her husband; the groom
in turn was warned that if he beat his wife,
65 he must take care not to injure her seriously.
For years it was a custom in Hungary for the
groom to give the bride a kick after the
marriage ceremony.

3. The *best* title for the passage would be

   (A) Marriage: Then and Now
   (B) Ritualistic Variations in Marriage
   (C) Choice of Mate in Marriage
   (D) Social Customs in Marriage: A Study of Symbolic Servitude
   (E) Polygamous and Monogamous Marriage Rites

4. According to the passage, which of the following statements would most likely be true?

   (A) In most modern societies marriage is based on love
   (B) Poor women in Assyria probably had great difficulty acquiring a mate
   (C) The honeymoon symbolizes early intertribal marriage
   (D) An officiating clergyman is required in most marriages
   (E) Some parts of a modern marriage ceremony are based on pagan rituals

5. The word EXOGAMOUS as used in lines 15 and 16 means

   (A) Marriage by consent
   (B) Marriage outside the tribe
   (C) Marriage within a particular group
   (D) Marriage by force
   (E) Marriage by arrangement

6. Which of the following statements is <u>not</u> supported by the passage?

   (A) Neither love nor happiness was expected in a Zulu marriage
   (B) The wedding ring symbolizes the restriction of marriage
   (C) The honeymoon symbolizes marriage by capture
   (D) The dowry symbolizes marriage by purchase
   (E) Women in developing countries accept the subjugation of marriage

Exercise C: Humanities

With the exception of Falstaff, all of Shakespeare's characters are what we call marrying
men. Mercutio would have come to the same
end in the long run. Even Iago had a wife,
5 and, what is far stranger, he was jealous. People like Jacques and the Fool in *Lear,* although we can hardly imagine they would ever
marry, kept single out of a cynical humor or
for a broken heart, and not, as we do nowa-
10 days, from a spirit of incredulity and prefer-

ence for the single state. For that matter, if you turn to George Sand's French version of *As You Like It,* you will find Jacques marries Celia just as Orlando marries Rosalind.

15   At least there seems to have been much less hesitation over marriage in Shakespeare's days; and what hesitation there was was of a laughing sort. But in modern comedies the heroes are not one-quarter so confident. And I
20   take this diffidence as a proof of how sincere their terror is. They know they are only human after all; they know what pitfalls lie about their feet; and how the shadow of matrimony waits, resolute and awful, at the crossroads.
25   They would wish to keep their liberty; but if that may not be, why, God's will be done! . . . They look forward to marriage much in the same way as they prepare themselves for death: each seems inevitable; each is a great
30   Perhaps, and a leap into the dark, for which he has specially to harden his heart.
(Robert Louis Stevenson, *Virginibus Puerisque*)

7. The best title for this passage would be

(A) "To marry or not to marry . . . that is the question"
(B) The state of marriage in Shakespeare's plays
(C) The changing attitude toward marriage in drama
(D) One writer's views on the state of marriage
(E) Reasons for marriage

8. The writer's attitude in the passage is best described as

(A) Unqualified endorsement
(B) Healthy skepticism
(C) Scholarly disapproval
(D) Apathetic acceptance
(E) Analytical objectivity

9. We can infer from the information given in the passage that the attitude toward marriage exhibited in more modern plays is one of

(A) Unqualified acceptance
(B) Inevitable acceptance
(C) Confident acceptance
(D) Unqualified avoidance
(E) Complete disinterest

10. The passage is developed principally by means of

(A) Examples
(B) Definition
(C) Anecdotes
(D) Cause and effect
(E) Contrast

Vocabulary Builder

Follow the instructions for each of the exercises. Answer keys are provided at the end of the vocabulary builder section. Before doing the exercises, familiarize *yourself with the* 15 Key Prefixes, 16 Important Roots, 14 Key Suffixes, *and the* Essential Words.

15 Key Prefixes

1. ab, a, abs .... *away, from* (Lat.)
2. ambi .... *both, around* (Lat.)
3. circum .... *around* (Lat.)
4. dia .... *through, across* (Gr.)
5. endo .... *inside, within* (Gr.)
6. hetero .... *other, different* (Gr.)
7. holo .... *whole, entire* (Gr.)
8. homo .... *same* (Gr.)
9. infra .... *beneath, below* (Lat.)
10. pan, panto .... *all, every* (Gr.)
11. par(a) .... *beside, beyond, aside from* (Gr.)
12. poly .... *many* (Gr.)
13. prot(o) .... *first, original* (Gr.)
14. retro .... *backward; back* (Lat.)
15. ultra .... *beyond* (Lat.)

16 Important Roots

1. anthrop .... *man, mankind* (Gr.)
2. bene, bon .... *good, well* (Lat.)
3. ced, cess .... *go, yield* (Lat.)
4. gam .... *marriage* (Gr.)
5. gloss, glot(t) .... *tongue, language* (Gr.)
6. loqu, locut .... *speak* (Lat.)
7. pel(l), puls .... *drive, push* (Lat.)
8. pol, polis .... *city, state* (Gr.)
9. port .... *carry* (Lat.)
10. pyr .... *fire* (Gr.)
11. sent, sens .... *feel, think* (Lat.)
12. sequ, secut .... *follow* (Lat.)
13. simil, simul .... *like* (Lat.)
14. tract .... *draw, drag* (Lat.)
15. verb .... *word, verb* (Lat.)
16. vert, vers .... *turn* (Lat.)

14 Key Suffixes

Suffixes indicating smallness or lessening

cle, cule .... as in *article, particle, globule*
et, ette .... as in *dinette, palette, coronet*
en .... as in *kitten, chicken*
let .... as in *leaflet, bracelet, streamlet*
ling .... as in *duckling, darling*
ock .... as in *hillock, bullock*

Suffixes indicating the receiver of an action

ee .... as in *legatee, trustee, referee*

ar(er) .... one who: as in *scholar, farmer*
ant(ent) .... one who, that which: as in *tenant*
ard .... one who: as in *coward, sluggard*
eer, ier .... one who: as in *charioteer, brigadier*
ess .... a woman who: as in *authoress, countess*
or .... one who: as in *actor, sailor*
ster .... one who: as in *gamester, songster*

Essential Words—Human Relations

1. Beneficent—*(Adj)* doing good
2. Benevolent—*(Adj)* desiring to do good
3. Cynical—*(Adj)* doubting goodness of motive
4. Deportment—*(N)* conduct
5. Diffidence—*(N)* shyness, timidity
6. Emulate—*(V)* to try to equal or surpass; to rival successfully
7. Estrangement—*(N)* a turning away in feeling; becoming distant or unfriendly
8. Formidable—*(Adj)* fearful
9. Iconoclast—*(N)* attacker of cherished beliefs; rebel
10. Importunate—*(Adj)* asking repeatedly; annoyingly persistent
11. Interlocutor—*(N)* person who takes part in a conversation or dialog
12. Loquacious—*(Adj)* talkative
13. Obsequious—*(Adj)* polite or obedient for hope of gain or from fear; servile, fawning
14. Polygamy—*(N)* practice of having many spouses at one time
15. Subjugation—*(N)* state of being subdued or conquered

Essential Words—World of Practical Affairs

1. Abstemious—*(Adj)* moderate in eating, drinking, etc.
2. Adjudicate—*(V)* to decree or pass judgment
3. Arduous—*(Adj)* difficult, steep, severe
4. Cant—*(N)* insincere virtuous talk; special jargon
5. Cosmopolitan—*(Adj)* worldly
6. Covert—*(Adj)* secret or covered
7. Dictum—*(N)* a formal comment; authoritative opinion
8. Holocaust—*(N)* great destruction, esp. by fire
9. Megalopolis—*(N)* a large metropolitan area
10. Novice—*(N)* beginner; one just received into a religious order
11. Panacea—*(N)* cure-all
12. Retroactive—*(Adj)* applying also to the past
13. Semitic—*(Adj)* having to do with Semites or their languages
14. Spurious—*(Adj)* not genuine
15. Tumult—*(N)* disturbance, commotion, or uproar

Essential Words—Aesthetic-Philosophical

1. Antithesis—*(N)* direct opposite
2. Colloquial—*(Adj)* appropriate to ordinary rather than formal speech or writing
3. Cynicism—*(N)* a doubting, sneering quality or disposition
4. Embodiment—*(N)* person or thing symbolizing an idea or quality
5. Epithet—*(N)* descriptive term for a person or thing
6. Epitome—*(N)* person or thing that is typical or representative of something
7. Felicity—*(N)* happiness
8. Inimical—*(Adj)* adverse, hostile
9. Misogamy—*(N)* hatred of marriage
10. Mitigate—*(V)* make milder, ease
11. Ostensible—*(Adj)* apparent, seeming
12. Pantheism—*(N)* belief that God and the universe are identical
13. Parochial—*(Adj)* narrow; limited
14. Prodigious—*(Adj)* huge; wonderful
15. Tractable—*(Adj)* easily managed

Essential Words—Science Related

1. Adventitious—*(Adj)* added from the outside
2. Anthropology—*(N)* science of study of mankind
3. Appendage—*(N)* subordinate attached part
4. Assimilate—*(V)* absorb, or become absorbed; merge
5. Constituent—*(Adj)* being a part; component; *(N)* representing voters
6. Heterogenic—*(Adj)* unlike, varied
7. Insensate—*(Adj)* without feeling
8. Interpose—*(V)* place between, intervene
9. Multifarious—*(Adj)* many and varied
10. Pandemic—*(Adj)* spread over an entire country, continent, or the world
11. Pyretic—*(Adj)* of or having to do with fever
12. Sinologist—*(N)* one who studies the Chinese people, culture, etc.
13. Venerate—*(V)* to revere
14. Vertiginous—*(Adj)* whirling; rotary; revolving
15. Vortex—*(N)* whirling movement or mass

Exercise 1—Roots

Match the Root in Column A with its meaning in Column B.

Column A		Column B	
1.	anthrop	(A)	man, mankind
2.	bene, bon	(B)	good, well
3.	ced, cess	(C)	word, verb
4.	gam	(D)	speak
5.	gloss, glot(t)	(E)	go, yield
6.	loqu, locut	(F)	follow
7.	pel(l), puls	(G)	carry
8.	pol, polis	(H)	like
9.	port	(I)	draw, drag
10.	pyr	(J)	marriage
11.	sent, sens	(K)	drive, push

12.	sequ, secut	(L)	city, state
13.	simil, simul	(M)	feel, think
14.	tract	(N)	turn
15.	verb	(O)	tongue, language
16.	vert, vers	(P)	fire

1. _____   5. _____   9. _____   13. _____

2. _____   6. _____   10. _____   14. _____

3. _____   7. _____   11. _____   15. _____

4. _____   8. _____   12. _____   16. _____

Exercise 2—Prefixes

Match the Prefix in Column A with its meaning in Column B.

Column A		Column B	
1.	a, ab, abs	(A)	away, from
2.	ambi	(B)	both, around
3.	circum	(C)	beneath, below
4.	dia	(D)	around
5.	endo	(E)	through, across
6.	infra	(F)	all, every
7.	hetero	(G)	many
8.	holo	(H)	beyond
9.	homo	(I)	backward; back
10.	pan, panto	(J)	same
11.	par (a)	(K)	other, different
12.	poly	(L)	first, original
13.	prot(o)	(M)	inside, within
14.	retro	(N)	beside, beyond, aside from
15.	ultra	(O)	whole, entire

1. _____   6. _____   11. _____

2. _____   7. _____   12. _____

3. _____   8. _____   13. _____

4. _____   9. _____   14. _____

5. _____   10. _____   15. _____

Exercise 3

For each of the key words in Exercise 3 select from the list below one word that is most nearly the same in meaning to the key word and one word that is most nearly opposite to the key word. The first one is done for you.

Synonyms	Antonyms
aftermath	attraction
attentive	benefactor
aversion	commanding
bigamy	concise
blessing	constant

43

charitable	curse
chatter	dispersion
consent	fireproof
conversation	foundation
cynic	intensify
defamation	monogamy
difference	monolingual
diminish	monolog
docile	neglectful
flames	real
foolish	sameness
multilingual	silent
plausible	stingy
pretend	stubborn
prior	subsequent
servile	thoughtful
spontaneous	unbelievable
stretch	veneration
unstable	wise
wordy	withhold

1. Accede
KEY WORD

ac	ced	
prefix(es)	root	suffix(es)

to yield	to give one's assent
literal meaning	definition

consent	withhold
synonym	antonym

2. Advertent
KEY WORD

ad	vert	ent
prefix(es)	root	suffix(es)

to turn toward	paying attention; heedful
literal meaning	definition

synonym	antonym

3. Antecedent
KEY WORD

ante	ced	ent
prefix(es)	root	suffix(es)

to go before	coming before in time, order, logic
literal meaning	definition

synonym	antonym

44

4. Benediction
KEY WORD

	bene/dict	ion
prefix(es)	root	suffix(es)

to speak well	a blessing; an invocation at the end of a religious service
literal meaning	definition

synonym	antonym

5. Benevolent
KEY WORD

	bene/volen	
prefix(es)	root	suffix(es)

to wish well	inclined to do good
literal meaning	definition

synonym	antonym

6. Dissimilarity
KEY WORD

dis	similis	ity
prefix(es)	root	suffix(es)

unlike	quality of being distinct
literal meaning	definition

synonym	antonym

7. Impulsive
KEY WORD

im	puls	ive
prefix(es)	root	suffix(es)

impel	impelling; driving forward
literal meaning	definition

synonym	antonym

8. Insensate
KEY WORD

in	sens	ate
prefix(es)	root	suffix(es)

not gifted with sense	lacking sensibility
literal meaning	definition

synonym	antonym

9. Interlocution
KEY WORD

inter	locut	ion
prefix(es)	root	suffix(es)

speak between	speech between two or more persons
literal meaning	definition

synonym	antonym

10. Loquacious
KEY WORD

	loqu	(aci) ous
prefix(es)	root	suffix(es)

to speak	very talkative
literal meaning	definition

synonym	antonym

11. Misanthrope
KEY WORD

mis	anthrop	
prefix(es)	root	suffix(es)

hating mankind	person who distrusts mankind
literal meaning	definition

synonym	antonym

46

12. Obloquy
KEY WORD

ob	loqu	y
prefix(es)	root	suffix(es)

to speak against	abusively detractive language
literal meaning	definition

synonym	antonym

13. Obsequious
KEY WORD

ob	sequi	ous
prefix(es)	root	suffix(es)

to follow	compliance
literal meaning	definition

synonym	antonym

14. Polygamy
KEY WORD

poly	gam	y
prefix(es)	root	suffix(es)

many spouses	having more than one wife at the same time
literal meaning	definition

synonym	antonym

15. Polyglot
KEY WORD

poly	glot	
prefix(es)	root	suffix(es)

many tongues	person who speaks many languages
literal meaning	definition

synonym	antonym

47

16. Pyre
KEY WORD

prefix(es)	**pyr** root	suffix(es)
fire literal meaning	**any pile of combustibles** definition	
synonym	antonym	

17. Recede
KEY WORD

re prefix(es)	**cede** root	suffix(es)
to go back literal meaning	**withdraw** definition	
synonym	antonym	

18. Repulsive
KEY WORD

re prefix(es)	**puls** root	**ive** suffix(es)
drive back literal meaning	**arousing disgust** definition	
synonym	antonym	

19. Sequel
KEY WORD

prefix(es)	**sequ** root	suffix(es)
follow literal meaning	**something that follows** definition	
synonym	antonym	

20. Simulate
KEY WORD

prefix(es)	simul	ate
	root	suffix(es)

together with	to imitate
literal meaning	definition

synonym	antonym

21. Tractable
KEY WORD

prefix(es)	tract	able
	root	suffix(es)

capable of drawing, pulling	easily managed
literal meaning	definition

synonym	antonym

22. Traction
KEY WORD

prefix(es)	tract	ion
	root	suffix(es)

the act of drawing, pulling	a pulling or drawing
literal meaning	definition

synonym	antonym

23. Verbose
KEY WORD

prefix(es)	verb	ose
	root	suffix(es)

word	using an excessive number of words
literal meaning	definition

synonym	antonym

49

24. Verisimilitude
KEY WORD

prefix(es)	verus/similis	suffix(es)
	root	

to seem real	having the appearance of being true or real
literal meaning	definition

synonym	antonym

25. Vertiginous
KEY WORD

prefix(es)	vertig	inous
	root	suffix(es)

whirling	dizzy; unstable
literal meaning	definition

synonym	antonym

Exercise 4—Root Words and Meanings

Fill in the blanks with the correct words.

1. The root _____ is found in *beneficence*.

    BENEFICENCE means _____.

2. The root _____ is found in *elocution*.

    ELOCUTION means _____ .

3. The root _____ is found in *impulsion*.

    IMPULSION means _____ .

4. The root _____ is found in *metropolis*.

    METROPOLIS means _____ .

5. The root _____ is found in *polygamous*.

    POLYGAMOUS means _____ .

6. The root _____ is found in *polyglot*.

    POLYGLOT means _____ .

7. The root _____ is found in *pyrotechnic*.

    PYROTECHNIC means _____ .

8. The root _____ is found in *reversion*.

    REVERSION means _____ .

9. The root _____ is found in *sensitivity*.

   SENSITIVITY means _____ .

10. The root _____ is found in *sequential*.

   SEQUENTIAL means _____ .

Exercise 5—Essential Words

Match each word in Column A with its definition in Column B.

Column A

1. antithesis
2. arduous
3. beneficent
4. diffidence
5. formidable
6. iconoclast
7. inimical
8. mitigate
9. retroactive
10. tractable

Column B

(A) easily managed
(B) difficult, severe
(C) doing good
(D) applying to the past
(E) fearful
(F) shyness, timidity
(G) adverse, severe
(H) direct opposite
(I) make milder, ease
(J) rebel

1. _____

2. _____

3. _____

4. _____

5. _____

6. _____

7. _____

8. _____

9. _____

10. _____

Exercise 6—Opposites

Match each word in Column A with the word must nearly opposite in Column B.

Column A

1. arduous
2. beneficence
3. diffidence
4. heterogeneous
5. iconoclast
6. loquacious
7. ostensible
8. pandemic
9. polygamous
10. tractable

Column B

(A) selfishness
(B) unmanageable
(C) silent
(D) monogamous
(E) real
(F) confined
(G) brashness
(H) easy
(I) traditionalist
(J) homogeneous

1. _____

2. _____

3. _____

6. _____

7. _____

8. _____

4. _____   9. _____

5. _____   10. _____

Exercise 7—Sentence Completion

Complete the sentences in Column B by filling in the blank with the word from Column A.

Column A

1. antithesis
2. arduous
3. constituent
4. formidable
5. impulsive
6. inimical
7. interposed
8. ostensible
9. pyrotechnic
10. tractable

Column B

1. Dogs are more _____ than mules.

2. Her _____ purpose was to borrow sugar, but she really wanted to see my new refrigerator.

3. She _____ an objection at this point.

4. The _____ child spent all of his money on candy.

5. I was greatly surprised by her _____ response to my suggestion.

6. The champion boxer was considered to be a _____ opponent.

7. The _____ task of alphabetizing the index cards left the clerk fatigued.

8. The _____ display on the Fourth of July was a sight to behold.

9. Hate is the _____ of love.

10. Flour, sugar, and eggs are _____ parts of cakes.

Vocabulary Check Test

(Answers will be reviewed in televised Verbal Lesson Two or by your classroom teacher.)

Part A

Choose the word or phrase most nearly opposite to the word in capital letters.

1. IMPULSIVE: (A) lavish   (B) normal   (C) pliable
                  (D) romantic   (E) prudent

2. CONSECUTIVE: (A) straight   (B) flowing   (C) uneven
                  (D) interrupted (E) regular

3. FELICITY: (A) distress   (B) dubiety   (C) fruitfulness
                  (D) cruelty   (E) ardor

4. ACCEDE: (A) declare   (B) happen sooner (C) exalt
                  (D) release   (E) withhold

5. MISANTHROPE: (A) cynic   (B) misogamist (C) ruffian
                  (D) benefactor (E) moralist

6. VERISIMILITUDE: (A) metaphor   (B) inconceivability (C) authenticity
                   (D) misstatement (E) autograph

52

7. EPITOME:
   (A) enlargement   (B) compendium   (C) epoch
   (D) tenet   (E) scholarship

8. OBLOQUY:
   (A) commentary   (B) stipulation   (C) commendation
   (D) pliancy   (E) futurism

9. VERBOSE:
   (A) know-nothing   (B) laconic   (C) moderate
   (D) outrageous   (E) meticulous

10. SPURIOUS:
    (A) provincial   (B) uncouth   (C) vehement
    (D) authentic   (E) loyal

11. INSIPID:
    (A) sporadic   (B) interesting   (C) solvable
    (D) stable   (E) picturesque

12. ESTRANGEMENT:
    (A) affinity   (B) dignity   (C) frivolity
    (D) obstruction   (E) relative

13. ADVENTITIOUS:
    (A) intentional   (B) jocund   (C) solemn
    (D) symmetrical   (E) integral

14. EMULATION:
    (A) obedience   (B) apathy   (C) monotone
    (D) setback   (E) grin

15. PYRE:
    (A) nymph   (B) impurity   (C) incombustibility
    (D) intensity   (E) glacier

Part B

From the list below choose the word that best completes the analogy by expressing a relationship similar to that expressed in the original pair.

(A) countenance   (F) covertness
(B) vertiginous   (G) loquaciousness
(C) megalopolis   (H) novice
(D) deportment   (I) appendage
(E) vortex   (J) polyglot

16. Planet: solar system:: city: _____

17. Washing machine: agitative:: gyroscope: _____

18. Sigh: voice:: grimace: _____

19. Disposition: temperament:: behavior: _____

20. Earth: rotation:: tornado: _____

21. Prestidigitator: magician:: linguist: _____

22. Shark: fin:: body: _____

23. Silence: verbosity:: reticence: _____

24. Supreme Court: equity:: Central Intelligence Agency: _____

25. Symposium: specialist:: training program: _____

53

Part C

From the list below select the words that best fit the meaning or context of the sentence.

(1) arduous
(2) assurance
(3) cosmopolitan
(4) dissimilarity
(5) homogeneous

(6) impulsive
(7) indicative
(8) misgiving
(9) parochial
(10) scurrilous

26. Although the substance of American and British English is essentially _____, yet some _____ exists.

27. The moment the _____ climb exhausted us, we regretted our hasty _____ decision.

28. A listener with a _____ viewpoint often fails to experience the _____ character of the world's great music.

29. His _____ behavior was not too surprising to people who knew his family. Vulgar language was _____ of his parents' verbal expression.

30. If a man begins with certainty, he shall end in doubt; but if he begins with _____ he shall end in _____.

Verbal
Lesson
Three

Simulated Verbal Examination

Time—30 Minutes

(The answers to the examination will be reviewed in televised Verbal Lesson Three or by your classroom teacher.)

Segment 1: Opposites

Select the word that is most nearly opposite in meaning to the word or phrase in capital letters. Consider any fine shades of meaning that may exist.

Example:

HOT: (A) green   (B) river   (C) cold
        (D) above   (E) sweet

	A	B	C	D	E
	○	○	●	○	○

1. IMPETUOUS: (A) fictitious   (B) engaged   (C) bellicose
                (D) calm   (E) infantile

2. VEXATION: (A) pleasure   (B) fiasco   (C) information
                (D) modification   (E) gesture

3. CURSORY: (A) selfish   (B) foul   (C) religious
                (D) fraternal (E) thorough

4. ALACRITY: (A) sheen   (B) untruthfulness   (C) apathy
                (D) speed   (E) fluency

5. IGNOMINIOUS: (A) unidentified   (B) clever   (C) honorable
                   (D) suspicious   (E) realistic

6. ENRAPTURE: (A) repel   (B) expose   (C) reminisce
                 (D) praise   (E) surrender

7. IRRESOLUTE: (A) blunt   (B) eccentric   (C) contagious
                  (D) grisly   (E) determined

8. DESULTORY: (A) fabricated   (B) alluring   (C) abusive
                 (D) methodical   (E) rapid

9. HEINOUS: (A) venial   (B) faddish   (C) tyrannical
               (D) slippery   (E) limited

10. INNOCUOUS: (A) logical   (B) silent   (C) fictitious
                  (D) hurtful   (E) noticeable

55

11. ACRIMONY: (A) compromise   (B) darkness   (C) gentleness
                                   (D) ceremony   (E) payment

12. PROLIX: (A) concise   (B) intemperate (C) stiff
                                   (D) doubtful   (E) obese

13. COMPENDIUM: (A) reference   (B) convention   (C) irregularity
                                   (D) disruption   (E) enlargement

14. PUGNACIOUS: (A) supportive   (B) eager   (C) indigent
                                   (D) conciliatory (E) gaunt

15. SUPERCILIOUS: (A) flaccid   (B) bare   (C) dull
                                   (D) popular   (E) respectful

Segment 2: Sentence Completion

The blanks in each sentence indicate omitted words. Select the word or words that best fit the meaning of the entire sentence and should be inserted in the blank.

Example:

On a small farm in an arid climate one should not grow crops that need considerable _____ or

_____ to ripen.

(A) fertilizer — attention   (B) space — water
(C) sun — air   (D) tilling — harvesting
(E) weeding — insecticides

                                           A   B   C   D   E
                                           ○   ●   ○   ○   ○

16. The intricate _____ of a dictionary rests on the basic blueprint of its entries.

    (A) organization   (B) etymology
    (C) synonyms   (D) architecture
    (E) spelling

17. _____ is truth in action.

    (A) retribution   (B) obedience
    (C) absurdity   (D) learning
    (E) justice

18. His shrewd compromise at the crucial moment of the debate showed his great _____.

    (A) insecurity   (B) sagacity
    (C) generosity   (D) appeal
    (E) nobility

19. Waving one's arms in a _____ attempt to rise off the ground must lead to _____ results.

    (A) fulfilling — exaggerated   (B) horrendous — aeronautic
    (C) fruitless — worthless   (D) satisfactory — imaginative
    (E) scientific — enterprising

20. As a politician he was no _____, keeping to the party line on all vital issues.

    (A) partisan   (B) bungler
    (C) maverick   (D) campaigner
    (E) mediator

21. The use of _____ may subdue for a moment, but a nation is not governed which is perpetually _____.

    (A) elections — imprisoned   (B) oration — free
    (C) free speech — arguing   (D) logic — voting
    (E) force — conquered

22. Some of America's best writers, enraptured with regional speech, felt that in _____ they might find the _____ of the nation.

    (A) homogeneity — uniformity   (B) simpleness — bewilderment
    (C) foreigners — extremity   (D) local custom — essence
    (E) mountainous areas — toughness

23. People must learn to balance the _____ of "doing one's own thing" against the _____ it might cause to others.

    (A) wrong — pain   (B) personal rewards — hurt
    (C) freedom — compliance   (D) jubilation — mockery
    (E) honesty — hypocrisy

24. In recent years, those editors who compile anthologies for students of language have _____ popular usage by encouraging the broadest possible definitions.

    (A) confined   (B) confirmed
    (C) regulated   (D) decreased
    (E) ridiculed

25. We feed the _____ with decay and refuse, but it gives us back life and beauty for our _____.

    (A) cities — building   (B) mind — reading
    (C) soil — rubbish   (D) air — eyes
    (E) ocean — pollution

Segment 3: Analogies

Each question below contains a related pair of words or phrases followed by five lettered pairs of words or phrases. Select the answer that best expresses a relationship similar to that expressed in the original pair.

Example:
PURSUE: CATCH::

(A) occur: happen   (B) eat: drink
(C) track: overtake   (D) apprehend: chase
(E) contest: victory

A   B   C   D   E
○   ○   ●   ○   ○

26. SHEEP: MUTTON::

    (A) poultry: duck   (B) fish: filet
    (C) meat: stew   (D) steer: beef
    (E) bacon: pig

57

27. SUN: SOLAR SYSTEM::

   (A) Mars: Venus   (B) cosmos: universe
   (C) nucleus: atom   (D) moon: Earth
   (E) tooth: chew

28. PHILANTHROPY: GENEROSITY::

   (A) miserliness: magnanimity   (B) rich: poor
   (C) parsimony: frugality   (D) paragon: imperfection
   (E) chivalry: Middle Ages

29. LATENT: DISEASE::

   (A) latitude: globe   (B) person: quiescent
   (C) mask: actor   (D) First Aid: emergency
   (E) dormant: volcano

30. TRICKLE: FAUCET::

   (A) elevation: drawbridge   (B) channel: liquid
   (C) ebb: ocean   (D) seepage: drainpipe
   (E) flow: river

31. BELLIGERENT: PASSIVE::

   (A) intrepid: cringing   (B) condensed: thick
   (C) agitated: passionate   (D) amiable: friendly
   (E) confused: negligent

32. CRIME: CONVICTION::

   (A) affluence: gold   (B) diatribe: complaint
   (C) war: destruction   (D) distress: accident
   (E) agreement: arbitration

33. COLANDER: DRAINING::

   (A) chain: prohibit   (B) weigh: scale
   (C) mop: sponge   (D) spatula: flipping
   (E) griddle: toaster

34. LEAVE: LIBERTY::

   (A) drive: license   (B) stay: restriction
   (C) vote: freedom   (D) fence: place
   (E) flag: country

35. HERD: CATTLE::

   (A) pack: hounds   (B) litter: stable
   (C) pride: bears   (D) shoal: swarm
   (E) geese: gaggle

Segment 4: Reading Comprehension

The questions following each passage are based on its content. Your choice should be made on the basis of what is stated *or implied in the passage.*

One secret of Mr. Lincoln's remarkable
success in captivating the popular mind is un-

doubtedly an unconsciousness of self which
enables him, though under the necessity of
constantly using the capital "I," to do it
without any suggestion of egotism. There is no
single vowel which men's mouths can pro-
nounce with such difference of effect. That
which one shall hide away, as it were, behind
the substance of his discourse, or, if he bring
it to the front, shall use merely to give an
agreeable accent of individuality to what he
says, another shall make an offensive challenge to the self-satisfaction of all his hearers,
and an unwarranted intrusion upon each
man's sense of personal importance, irritating
every pore of his vanity, like a dry northeast
wind, to a goose-flesh of opposition and hos-
tility. Mr. Lincoln has never studied
Quintilian*; but he has, in the earnest simplicity and unaffected Americanism of his own
character, one art of oratory worth all the
rest. He forgets himself so entirely in his
object as to give his "I" the sympathetic
and persuasive effect of "We" with the great
body of his countrymen. Homely, dispassionate, showing all the rough-edged process
of his thought as it goes along, yet arriving at
his conclusions with an honest kind of every-
day logic, he is so eminently our representative man, that, when he speaks, it seems as
if the people were listening to their own
thinking aloud. The dignity of his thought
owes nothing to any ceremonial garb of words,
but to the manly movement that comes of
settled purpose and an energy of reason that
knows not what rhetoric means. He has always
addressed the intelligence of men, never
their prejudice, their passion, or their ignorance.

On the day of his death, this simple Western
attorney, who according to some part was a
vulgar joker, and whom the doctrinaires
among his own supporters accused of wanting
every element of statesmanship, was the most
absolute ruler in Christendom, and this solely
by the hold his good-humored sagacity had
laid on the hearts and understandings of his
countrymen. Nor was this all, for it appeared
that he had drawn the great majority, not
only of his fellow citizens, but of mankind
also, to his side. So strong and so persuasive
is honest manliness without a single quality
of romance or unreal sentiment to help it! A
civilian during times of the most captivating
military achievement, awkward, with no skill
in the lower technicalities of manners, he left

*A Roman instructor of public speaking and rhetoric.

59

behind him a fame beyond that of any conqueror, the memory of a grace higher than
60 that of outward person, and of a gentlemanliness deeper than mere breeding. Never before that startled April morning did such multitudes of men shed tears for the death of one they had never seen, as if with him a
65 friendly presence had been taken away from their lives, leaving them colder and darker. Never was funeral panegyric so eloquent as the silent look of sympathy which strangers exchanged when they met on that day. Their
70 common manhood had lost a kinsman.
(James Russell Lowell, *Abraham Lincoln*)

36. The author's primary purpose is to

(A) Describe the sorrow felt by citizens after Lincoln's death
(B) Explain Lincoln's greatness through an analysis of his character
(C) Defend Lincoln against those who criticized him
(D) Cite examples of Lincoln's good humor
(E) Relate Lincoln's simpleness to his crude upbringing

37. The author's tone suggests that his attitude toward Lincoln is one of

(A) Cautious acclaim   (B) Aloof disinterest
(C) Warm admiration   (D) Skeptical suspicion
(E) Casual interest

38. With which of these statements would the author agree?

(A) Lincoln had the unique quality of being able to stir his audience to a fever pitch with his impassioned speeches
(B) As an attorney, Lincoln benefited from his study of the great orators
(C) Although a vulgar joker at heart, Lincoln knew the boundaries of propriety and never intentionally embarrassed himself or others
(D) Lincoln's simple logic and speech disguised the thoughts of a truly great intellectual and man of learning
(E) Although awkward and mannerless at times, Lincoln's popularity resulted from his good-humored wisdom and honest manliness

39. When the writer describes Lincoln thought as owing "nothing to any ceremonial garb of words" he implies that Lincoln's speech was

(A) Simple   (B) Hesitant
(C) Rigidly formal (D) Poetic
(E) Redundant

40. We can infer from the ideas in the passage that

(A) Lincoln's death was mourned only in America
(B) Lincoln knew little of military strategy
(C) Lincoln was a passionate orator
(D) Lincoln had a vulgar sense of humor
(E) Lincoln was a poor statesman

If you want to know the length of a pedal pipe, you can calculate it in this way. There are some numbers you must remember, and one of them is this. You, in this country,
5 are subjected to the British insularity in

60

weights and measures; you use the foot and inch and yard. I am obliged to use that system, but I apologise to you for doing so, because it is so inconvenient, and I hope all Americans will do everything in their power to introduce the French metrical system. I hope the evil action performed by an English minister whose name I need not mention, because I do not wish to throw OBLOQUY on any one, may be remedied. He abrogated a useful rule, which for a short time was followed, and which I hope will soon be again enjoined, that the French metrical system be taught in all our national schools. I do not know how it is in America. The school system seems to be very admirable, and I hope the teaching of the metrical system will not be let slip in the American schools any more than the use of the globes. I say this seriously: I do not think anyone knows how seriously I speak of it. I look upon our English system as a wickedly brain-destroying piece of bondage under which we suffer. The reason why we continue to use it is the imaginary difficulty of making a change, and nothing else; but I do not think in America that any such difficulty should stand in the way of adopting so splendidly useful a reform.

I know the velocity of sound in feet per second. If I remember rightly, it is 1,089 feet per second in dry air at the freezing temperature, and 1,115 feet per second in air of what we would call moderate temperature, 59 or 60 degrees—(I do not know whether that temperature is ever attained in Philadelphia or not; I have had no experience of it, but people tell me it is sometimes 59 or 60 degrees in Philadelphia, and I believe them)—in round numbers let us call the speed 1,000 feet per second. Sometimes we call it a thousand musical feet per second, it saves trouble in calculating the length of organ pipes; the time of vibration in an organ pipe is the time it takes a vibration to run from one end to the other and back. In an organ pipe 500 feet long the period would be one per second; in an organ pipe 10 feet long the period would be 50 per second; in an organ pipe 20 feet long the period would be 25 per second at the time rate. Thus 25 per second, and 50 per second of frequencies correspond to the periods of organ pipes of 20 feet and 10 feet.

(Lord Kelvin, *The Wave Theory of Light*)

41. According to the passage, the time of vibration in an organ pipe 50 feet long in round numbers would be

(A) 100 per second (B) 1,000 per second
(C) 1 per second (D) 10 per second
(E) ½ per second

42. It can be inferred that the author's concern with the current system of measurement is that of

(A) An uninformed commentator (B) An approving scientist
(C) A wary critic (D) An irate and critical scientist
(E) An annoyed observer

43. The style of this passage can best be described as

(A) Argumentative (B) Explanatory
(C) Contemplative (D) Rhetorical
(E) Scholarly

44. The author is primarily concerned with

(A) Criticizing the British school system in their teaching of an unwieldy system of measurements
(B) Urging the American school systems to use the metric system
(C) Illustrating by example how the velocity of sound is affected by the length of an organ pipe
(D) Illustrating the importance for students to remember the velocity of sound in feet per second
(E) Illustrating how a "rounded" system of measurement makes convenient the calculation of the time of vibration in an organ pipe

45. The writer uses the word OBLOQUY in line 14 to mean

(A) Obligation (B) Praise
(C) Excuse (D) Discredit
(E) Obscurity

Skill Builder—Reading Comprehension

Following each passage is a question or group of questions based on its content. Select the best answer to each question. The answers will be reviewed in televised Verbal Lesson Three or by your classroom teacher.

Exercise A: Historical

In certain remote corners of the Old World you may still sometimes stumble upon a small district which seems to have been forgotten amid the general tumult, and to have re-
5 mained stationary while everything around it was in motion. The inhabitants are for the most part extremely ignorant and poor; they take no part in the business of the country, and they are frequently oppressed by the
10 government; yet their countenances are generally placid, and their spirits light. In America I saw the freest and most enlightened men placed in the happiest circumstances that the world affords: it seemed to me as if a
15 cloud habitually hung upon their brow, and I thought them serious and almost sad even in their pleasures. The chief reason of this con-

trast is that the former do not think of the ills they endure—the latter are forever brooding over advantages they do not possess. It is strange to see with what feverish ardour the Americans pursue their own welfare; and to watch the vague dread that constantly torments them lest they should not have chosen the shortest path which may lead to it. A native of the United States clings to this world's goods as if he were certain never to die; and he is so hasty in grasping at all within his reach that one would suppose he was constantly afraid of not living long enough to enjoy them. He clutches everything, he holds nothing fast, but soon loosens his grasp to pursue fresh gratifications.

In the United States a man builds a house to spend his latter years in it, and he sells it before the roof is on; he plants a garden, and lets it just as the trees are coming into bearing; he brings a field into tillage, and leaves other men to gather the crops; he embraces a profession, and gives it up; he settles in a place, which he soon afterward leaves, to carry his changeable longings elsewhere. If his private affairs leave him any leisure, he instantly plunges into the vortex of politics; and if at the end of a year of unremitting labour he finds he has a few days' vacation, his eager curiosity whirls him over the vast extent of the United States, and he will travel fifteen hundred miles in a few days to shake off his happiness. Death at length overtakes him, but it is before he is weary of his BOOTLESS CHASE of that complete felicity which is forever on the wing.

(Alexis de Tocqueville, *Democracy in America*)

1. The author is primarily interested in describing
   (A) The restless spirit of Americans in the midst of prosperity
   (B) The effects of freedom
   (C) The provincial life of Americans
   (D) The mobility of American citizens
   (E) American concern for materialism

2. Which of the following statements about Americans is supported by the passage?
   (A) Most are ignorant and poor
   (B) Most are unconcerned about their misfortune
   (C) Most are a contented people
   (D) Most find happiness before death
   (E) Most are eager to possess as much as possible in the shortest period of time

3. In presenting his ideas, the author uses all of the following methods except
   (A) Observation   (B) Generalization
   (C) Personal endorsement (D) Logical implication
   (E) Illustrative incidents

63

4. The author's use of the phrase BOOTLESS CHASE in lines 51 and 52 could best be interpreted to mean

(A) Automobile journey   (B) Attempted smuggling
(C) Repeated successes   (D) Fruitless pursuit
(E) Prolonged walks

Exercise B: Scientific

(Reprinted with permission from *Science 80*)

The world is an illusion created by a conspiracy of our senses that make it seem three-dimensional. This three-dimensional sense of reality holds up because when one pets the dog or bites into an apple, these objects fill three palpable dimensions in space—height, width, and breadth. For most people, those three dimensions define all of physical reality.

But physicists have superceded that. Early in this century, Albert Einstein went beyond three dimensions to delve into the four-dimensional world of space-time. He derived some of the rules that govern its behavior, rules that seem to defy common sense. As incredible as they seemed at first, the rules—like $E=mc^2$—ultimately were used to release atomic energy.

Now from the research of theoretical mathematician Roger Penrose of England's Oxford University, a new, multidimensional universe is emerging—one just as strange as the world Einstein uncovered, just as counter-intuitive, and possibly just as significant. Penrose, a mathematical puzzle wizard as well as a theoretician, reaches into the subatomic world that Einstein's theory does not describe to try to construct a model of the universe using basic building blocks he calls twistors.

Penrose's research arises partially in response to one of the most bothersome dichotomies in physics today: In all the mathematical calculations involving the macroscopic world, from designing toasters to calculating the distances to the farthest stars, real numbers are used. Even Einstein's theory of gravity, the general theory of relativity, uses only real numbers. But for the submicroscopic world of the atom, real numbers are inadequate. To solve the intricate equations of quantum theory, a different system of numbers called complex numbers is required.

Roger Penrose feels that this dichotomy is wrong. Since everything material is made of atoms, and all energy exists as discrete

bundles called quanta, and since both atoms
and quanta require the use of complex numbers instead of real numbers, Penrose feels
that all of our calculations about the universe should use complex numbers. But to do
this completely means reformulating all the
other major laws of physics—such as Einstein's theory of gravity and the laws that
describe electricity and magnetism—with
new mathematics that use complex numbers
instead of real numbers.

Penrose goes even further. At present the
space-time of our world is described in real
numbers. He thinks that perhaps even this is
wrong. Maybe the seemingly solid space-time
around us is just a real-world illusion of a
more complex universe that uses the logical
highly controlled system of complex numbers.
In an attempt to develop these ideas, Penrose
has created a conceptually new way of looking
at the universe: It is called twistor theory
and it uses complex numbers. From this he
hopes to produce a unified view of all physics
and thus create an entirely new vision of
reality.

Complex numbers are an essential aspect
of this new Penrosian universe. While some of
the math is standard, the important and
crucial part of Penrose's intuitive and courageous vision is the orderly nature of complex
numbers and its effect on his theory.
(Robert L. Forward)

5. The title that best expresses the ideas of the passage is

(A) A New, Multidimensional Universe
(B) The General Theory of Relativity
(C) Complex and Real Number Systems
(D) The Subatomic World
(E) The Imaginative World of Physicists

6. We can infer that Penrose's theories will be

(A) Readily accepted by the scientific community
(B) Easily tied in with Einstein's theories
(C) Placed in the same category as magic and legerdemain
(D) Cautiously received by the scientific community
(E) Based on standard mathematical formulas

7. Which of the following is most likely true of both Penrose and Einstein?

  I. The theories of both were counter-intuitive to the current thinking of the time
 II. Both men's theories use only real numbers
III. Both men's theories are relevant to the subatomic world

(A) I only
(C) I and III only
(E) I, II, and III

(B) I and II only
(D) II and III only

8. Which of the following best describes the author's attitude toward Penrose's theories?

(A) Prudent disbelief
(B) Suspicious skepticism
(C) Qualified optimism
(D) Impartial objectivity
(E) Arrogant disdain

Vocabulary Builder

Follow the instructions for each of the exercises. Answer keys are provided at the end of the vocabulary builder section. Before doing the exercise, familiarize *yourself with the* 10 Key Prefixes, 17 Important Roots, 10 Key Suffixes, *and the* Essential Words.

10 Key Prefixes

1. archae, archa[1] .... *ancient, primitive, first in time* (Gr.)

2. cata, cat, cath[2] .... *down, down from, away, against, completely, according to* (Gr.)

3. ec, ex .... *out of, away from* (Gr.)

4. ecto .... *outside of* (Gr.)

5. epi, ep[3] .... *upon, over, around, next to, in addition, after* (Gr.)

6. juxta .... *near, next* (Lat.)

7. ortho, orth[4] .... *straight, upright, correct, at right angles or perpendicular to* (Gr.)

8. preter .... *past, beyond* (Lat.)

9. summa, suprem, super .... *highest, above, over* (Lat.)

10. syn, syl, sy[5] .... *together, with, same, similar, union, fusion* (Gr.)

1. The prefix *archae* and *archa* and the root *arch* or *archi* can be traced to the same root meaning first or beginning. Through usage *archae* came to refer to *first in time* and *arch* came to refer to *first in rank or status*, leader or ruler.

2. *Cata* conveys six meanings: (1) down (catabolism); (2) down from (catalepsy); (3) away or off (catalectic); (4) against (category); (5) completely or thoroughly (catachresis); (6) according to (catechize).

3. *Epi* conveys six meanings: (1) upon (epiphyte); (2) over (epicenter); (3) around (epineurium); (4) next to (epicalyx); (5) in addition (epiphenomenon); (6) after (epigenesis).

4. *Ortho* conveys four meanings: (1) straight or upright (orthotropic); (2) at right angles or perpendicular to (orthorhombic); (3) correct or standard (orthography); (4) correction of deformities (orthopedics).

5. *Syn* conveys three meanings: (1) together or with (syndactyl); (2) same or similar (synchronize); (3) union, fusion, a joining together (synapse) (synapsis).

17 Important Roots

1. arch, archi .... *rule, govern* (Gr.)

2. celer .... *swift* (Lat.)

3. chron .... *time* (Gr.)

4. cid (cis) .... *kill, cut* (Lat.)

5. fin .... *end, limit, border* (Lat.)

6. fort (forc) .... *strong* (Lat.)

7. greg .... *flock, herd* (Lat.)

8. junc, jug[1] .... *join* (Lat.)

9. jur[2] .... *swear* (Lat.)
   just[3] .... *justice* (Lat.)
   juris[4] .... *law, right* (Lat.)
   judic[5] .... *judge, decide* (Lat.)

10. mund .... *world, earth* (Lat.)

11. pecu .... *money, private property, one's own* (Lat.)

12. psych .... *mind, soul, spirit* (Gr.)

13. reg (rig), rect .... *straighten, rule* (Lat.)

14. sol(i)[6] .... *alone* (Lat.)

15. som, somat .... *body* (Gr.)

16. therm .... *heat* (Gr.)

17. troph .... *nourish, grow* (Gr.)

1. *jug* from the Latin *jugare:* to join or yoke together. Thus, marriage joins or yokes together. To subjugate an enemy once meant to put him under yoke.

2. *jur* from the Latin jurare: to swear

3. *just* from the Latin justus: just

4. *juris* from the Latin jus: law

5. *judic* and other *jud* words from the Latin judex: judge

6. another *sol* means sun

10 Key Suffixes

Suffixes Indicating Place

ary .... indicating location, repository: as in *dictionary, apiary*

ery .... place, establishment: as in *nunnery, bakery, eatery*

Suffixes Indicating an Act, State, Quality, or Condition

acy .... indicating quality, state: as in *accuracy, delicacy*

al .... indicating action: as in *refusal, denial*

ance, ancy .... indicating action or state: as in *brilliance, buoyancy*

ation .... indicating result: as in *immigration, elation*

hood .... indicating state or quality: as in *brotherhood, knighthood*

ion, sion .... indicating state or condition: as in *remission, union*

ism .... indicating action, state, or condition: as in *plagiarism, barbarism*

ness .... indicating quality, state of: as in *sweetness, unpreparedness*

Essential Words—Human Relations

1. Acrimony—(N) sharpness; severity of temper or manner
2. Arduous—(Adj) difficult, steep, severe
3. Conjugal—(Adj) of marriage
4. Conspiracy—(N) a plot
5. Countenance—(N) appearance, face; encouragement
6. Ebullient—(Adj) overflowing with excitement; liveliness
7. Egotism—(N) talking chiefly of oneself
8. Facetious—(Adj) joking; not to be taken seriously
9. Fortitude—(N) patient courage
10. Gregarious—(Adj) fond of company
11. Intrepid—(Adj) very brave, fearless, courageous
12. Lecherous—(Adj) lustful, lewd
13. Rectitude—(N) upright character or conduct; honesty
14. Sagacity—(N) keen, sound judgment; mental acuteness
15. Truculent—(Adj) savage, cruel, fierce

Essential Words—World of Practical Affairs

1. Adjudication—(N) decision of a judge or court of law
2. Ambulatory—(Adj) able to walk
3. Banality—(N) commonplaceness, triteness, triviality
4. Cavort—(V) prance about
5. Discourse—(N) formal or extensive speech or writing
6. Eschew—(V) to abstain from; stand aloof from; shun
7. Insular—(Adj) narrow-minded, prejudiced
8. Jurisprudence—(N) Science of Law
9. Pannier—(N) a large wicker basket
10. Pecuniary—(Adj) of or having to do with money
11. Placid—(Adj) serene, peaceful
12. Stabilize—(V) make firm, prevent changes in
13. Tumult—(N) disturbance, commotion, or uproar
14. Unremitting—(Adj) never stopping or slackening
15. Volant—(Adj) flying or capable of flying—agile

Essential Words—Aesthetic-Philosophical

1. Bootless—(Adj) of no benefit or profit, useless
2. Cacophony—(N) a harsh, clashing sound, discord
3. Credo—(N) formula of belief
4. Definitive—(Adj) conclusive, final
5. Dichotomy—(N) division of a whole into two parts
6. Discursive—(Adj) rambling from one subject to another
7. Esoteric—(Adj) intended for a select few
8. Felicity—(N) great happiness, bliss
9. Gratification—(N) something that satisfies or pleases
10. Intrinsic—(Adj) belonging to a thing by its very nature
11. Intuitive—(Adj) acquired by intuition, instinctive, natural
12. Preternatural—(Adj) supernatural, abnormal
13. Rhetoric—(N) art of using words effectively in speaking or writing
14. Sacrosanct—(Adj) very holy, most sacred
15. Secular—(Adj) not religious or sacred; worldly

Essential Words—Science Related

1. Celerity—*(N)* speed, rapidity
2. Dimension—*(N)* magnitude
3. Ectogenous—*(Adj)* capable of development outside of the host (as are certain bacteria)
4. Epidermis—*(N)* outer layer of the skin
5. Homogeneity—*(N)* that which is of the same kind, nature, or character
6. Juxtapose—*(V)* put close together
7. Macroscopic—*(Adj)* visible to the naked eye
8. Orthography—*(N)* spelling or study of spelling
9. Ossification—*(N)* process of changing into bone; fixed in practice, custom, habit
10. Palpable—*(Adj)* obvious; tangible
11. Sloth—*(N)* laziness
12. Somatic—*(Adj)* of or having to do with the body
13. Syndrome—*(N)* signs and symptoms considered characteristic of a particular disease
14. Thermodynamics—*(N)* branch of physics that deals with relations between heat and other forms of energy, and of the conversion of one into the other
15. Tillage—*(N)* cultivated land, the cultivating of land

Exercise 1—Roots

Match the Root in Column A with its meaning in Column B.

Column A

1. arch, archi
2. celer
3. chron
4. cid (cis)
5. fin
6. fort (forc)
7. greg
8. junc, jug
9. jur, judic
10. mund
11. pecu
12. psych
13. reg (rig), rect
14. som, somat
15. therm
16. troph

Column B

(A) end, limit, border
(B) nourish, grow
(C) flock, herd
(D) straighten, rule
(E) rule, govern
(F) money, private property, one's own
(G) body
(H) strong
(I) world, earth
(J) join
(K) time
(L) kill, cut
(M) heat
(N) swear, judge, decide
(O) swift
(P) mind, soul, spirit

1. _____   5. _____   9. _____   13. _____

2. _____   6. _____   10. _____   14. _____

3. _____   7. _____   11. _____   15. _____

4. _____   8. _____   12. _____   16. _____

Exercise 2—Prefixes

Match the Prefix in Column A with its meaning in Column B.

Column A

1. archae, archa
2. cata, cat, cath
3. ec, ex
4. ecto
5. epi, ep
6. juxta
7. ortho, orth
8. preter
9. summ, suprem, super
10. syn, syl, sy

Column B

(A) outside of
(B) past, beyond
(C) ancient, primitive, first in time
(D) down, down from, away
(E) straight, upright, correct
(F) out of, away from
(G) near, next
(H) upon, over, around, next to
(I) highest, above, over
(J) together with, same

1. _____

2. _____

3. _____

4. _____

5. _____

6. _____

7. _____

8. _____

9. _____

10. _____

Exercise 3

For each of the key words in Exercise 3 select from the lists below one word that is most nearly the same in meaning to the key word and one word that is most nearly opposite to the key word. The first one is done for you.

Synonyms

1. abut
2. calamity
3. common
4. conclusive
5. dated
6. endurance
7. finale
8. fulfilled
9. fusion
10. insanity
11. lawlessness
12. limited
13. mistimed
14. monetary
15. physical
16. prolonged
17. rapidity
18. referee
19. renounce
20. selfishness
21. sociable
22. summary
23. supernatural
24. traditional
25. wither

Antonyms

affirm
altruism
boundless
grow
expansion
extraordinary
hermitic
iconoclastic
inconclusive
irregular
modern
order
ordinary
penniless
prologue
separate
separation
slowness
sound
spiritual
stability
unfinished
unresolved
weakness
well-timed

70

1. Abjure
KEY WORD

ab	jur(e)	
prefix(es)	root	suffix(es)

to swear away	swear to give up; retract formally
literal meaning	definition

renounce	affirm
synonym	antonym

2. Adjudicate
KEY WORD

ad	judic	ate
prefix(es)	root	suffix(es)

the characteristic of having to judge	to settle a case; pass judgment
literal meaning	definition

synonym	antonym

3. Anachronistic
KEY WORD

ana	chron	istic
prefix(es)	root	suffix(es)

reversed from the state of a particular time	anything out of its proper time
literal meaning	definition

synonym	antonym

4. Anarchy
KEY WORD

an	arch	y
prefix(es)	root	suffix(es)

without rule	a state of society without government or law
literal meaning	definition

synonym	antonym

5. Archaic
KEY WORD

archa		ic
prefix(es)	root	suffix(es)

pertaining to ancient times
literal meaning

belonging to a much earlier time;
no longer applicable
definition

synonym

antonym

6. Atrophy
KEY WORD

a	troph	y
prefix(es)	root	suffix(es)

without nourishment
literal meaning

to waste away
definition

synonym

antonym

7. Cataclysm
KEY WORD

cata	clysm	
prefix(es)	root	suffix(es)

to wash down
literal meaning

any violent upheaval; a great flood, earthquake, a sudden, violent change in the earth
definition

synonym

antonym

8. Celerity
KEY WORD

	celer	ity
prefix(es)	root	suffix(es)

pertaining to swiftness
literal meaning

swiftness of movement
definition

synonym

antonym

9. Chronic
KEY WORD

prefix(es)	chron	ic
	root	suffix(es)

pertaining to time	of long duration; lingering, as certain diseases
literal meaning	definition

synonym	antonym

10. Consummated
KEY WORD

con	summa(t)	ed
prefix(es)	root	suffix(es)

brought together to a peak	brought to completion
literal meaning	definition

synonym	antonym

11. Definitive
KEY WORD

de	fin(it)	ive
prefix(es)	root	suffix(es)

away from the end	precisely defined, decisive
literal meaning	definition

synonym	antonym

12. Egoism
KEY WORD

prefix(es)	ego	ism
	root	suffix(es)

state of being I	the habit of valuing everything only in reference to one's personal interest
literal meaning	definition

synonym	antonym

73

13. Epilogue
KEY WORD

epi	log(ue)	
prefix(es)	root	suffix(es)

to say in addition	a short addition or concluding section at the end of a literary work
literal meaning	definition

synonym	antonym

14. Finite
KEY WORD

	fin	ite
prefix(es)	root	suffix(es)

end	having limits or bounds
literal meaning	definition

synonym	antonym

15. Fortitude
KEY WORD

	fort	itude
prefix(es)	root	suffix(es)

state of being strong	patient courage under affliction
literal meaning	definition

synonym	antonym

16. Gregarious
KEY WORD

	greg	arious
prefix(es)	root	suffix(es)

having the quality of the herd	fond of the company of others; living in flocks or herds
literal meaning	definition

synonym	antonym

74

17. Juxtapose
KEY WORD

juxta	pose	
prefix(es)	root	suffix(es)

to place beside	put close together, place side by side
literal meaning	definition

synonym	antonym

18. Mundane
KEY WORD

	mund	ane
prefix(es)	root	suffix(es)

pertaining to the world	pertaining to everyday concerns; ordinary
literal meaning	definition

synonym	antonym

19. Orthodox
KEY WORD

ortho	dox	
prefix(es)	root	suffix(es)

correct opinion	customary; sound or correct in opinion; conforming to beliefs generally approved
literal meaning	definition

synonym	antonym

20. Pecuniary
KEY WORD

	pecu(n)	iary
prefix(es)	root	suffix(es)

pertaining to money	having to do with money; requiring the payment of money
literal meaning	definition

synonym	antonym

75

21. Preternatural
KEY WORD

preter	natur	al
prefix(es)	root	suffix(es)

pertaining to beyond nature	out of the ordinary course of nature
literal meaning	definition

synonym	antonym

22. Psychosis
KEY WORD

	psych	osis
prefix(es)	root	suffix(es)

a condition of the mind	a severe form of mental disorder that produces disruption of normal behavior
literal meaning	definition

synonym	antonym

23. Somatic
KEY WORD

	somat	ic
prefix(es)	root	suffix(es)

pertaining to the body	having to do with the body
literal meaning	definition

synonym	antonym

24. Synopsis
KEY WORD

syn	opsis	
prefix(es)	root	suffix(es)

to view together	a brief statement or outline of a subject; an abstract
literal meaning	definition

synonym	antonym

25. Synthesis

25. Synthesis
_____
KEY WORD

syn	thesis	
prefix(es)	root	suffix(es)

to place together
_____
literal meaning

combination of parts or elements
into a whole
_____
definition

_____
synonym

_____
antonym

Exercise 4—Root Words and Meanings

Fill in the blanks with the correct words.

1. The root _____ is found in *accelerate*.

    ACCELERATE means _____ .

2. The root _____ is found in *anarchy*.

    ANARCHY means _____ .

3. The root _____ is found in *atrophy*.

    ATROPHY means _____ .

4. The root _____ is found in *congregate*.

    CONGREGATE means _____ .

5. The root _____ is found in *fortification*.

    FORTIFICATION means _____ .

6. The root _____ is found in *juncture*.

    JUNCTURE means _____ .

7. The root _____ is found in *patricide*.

    PATRICIDE means _____ .

5. The root _____ is found in *psychosis*.

    PSYCHOSIS means _____ .

9. The root _____ is found in *rectify*.

    RECTIFY means _____ .

10. The root _____ is found in *thermostat*.

    THERMOSTAT means _____ .

Exercise 5—Essential Words

Match each word in Column A with its definition in Column B.

Column A

1. acrimony
2. banality
3. cacophony
4. celerity
5. ossification
6. palpable
7. pannier
8. sacrosanct
9. truculent
10. volant

Column B

(A) savage, cruel, fierce
(B) flying, or capable of flying
(C) a commonplace remark, triteness
(D) process of changing into bone
(E) large wicker basket
(F) obvious, tangible
(G) sharpness, severity of temper
(H) a harsh clashing sound
(I) very holy, most sacred
(J) speed, rapidity

1. _____

2. _____

3. _____

4. _____

5. _____

6. _____

7. _____

8. _____

9. _____

10. _____

Exercise 6—Antonyms

Match each word in Column A with the word must nearly opposite in Column B.

Column A

1. ambulatory
2. bootless
3. egotism
4. insular
5. intrepid
6. placid
7. preternatural
8. secular
9. sloth
10. tillage

Column B

(A) normal
(B) ambition
(C) bedridden
(D) useful
(E) religious
(F) fearful
(G) broad-minded
(H) modesty
(I) excitable
(J) wilderness

1. _____

2. _____

3. _____

4. _____

5. _____

6. _____

7. _____

8. _____

9. _____

10. _____

Exercise 7—Sentence Completion

Complete the sentences in Column B by filling in the blank with the correct word from Column A.

Column A	Column B
1. countenance	1. She appealed to the Supreme Court for a _____ answer.
2. definitive	2. He left the religious school to receive a _____ education.
3. egotism	3. The artist displayed an _____ understanding of color.
4. gregarious	4. No one shared his _____ prejudices.
5. insular	5. The cry of "fire" caused a _____ in the theater.
6. intuitive	6. The family maintained an _____ vigilance at the bedside of the patient.
7. secular	7. His _____ keeps him from engaging in sports.
8. sloth	8. They gave _____ to our plans, but no active help.
9. tumult	9. His _____ kept him from having friends.
10. unremitting	10. Hermits are not _____.

Vocabulary Check Test

(Answers will be reviewed in televised Verbal Lesson Three or by your classroom teacher.)

Part A

Choose the word or phrase most nearly opposite to the word in capital letters.

1. JUXTAPOSE: (A) justify (B) delete (C) separate
(D) request (E) oppose

2. PRETERNATURAL: (A) normal (B) guarded (C) artificial
(D) judicial (E) unfavorable

3. ATROPHIED: (A) awarded (B) flourished (C) inattentive
(D) obstructed (E) engraved

4. PSYCHOSIS: (A) fallacy (B) lunacy (C) travesty
(D) saline (E) sanity

5. FORTITUDE: (A) armory (B) courage (C) impatience
(D) resignation (E) turmoil

6. ICONOCLAST: (A) traditionalist (B) glazier (C) native
(D) pagan (E) villain

7. PLACID: (A) clear (B) weak (C) cautious
(D) disturbed (E) flowing

8. UNREMITTING: (A) relentless (B) unpaid (C) easing
(D) sagacious (E) everlasting

9. PERJURY: (A) eccentricity (B) benefit (C) justice
(D) perversion (E) veracity

| 10. ARCHAIC: | (A) fun-loving | (B) modern | (C) slippery |
| | (D) microscopic | (E) crumbling | |

| 11. ELABORATE: | (A) simple | (B) controversial | (C) expensive |
| | (D) curable | (E) factual | |

| 12. CHRONIC: | (A) aged | (B) tactful | (C) timely |
| | (D) communicable | (E) acute | |

| 13. DEFINITIVE: | (A) implied | (B) reckless | (C) tentative |
| | (D) logical | (E) foolish | |

| 14. AUDACITY: | (A) softness | (B) simplicity | (C) retort |
| | (D) timidity | (E) prowess | |

| 15. SOMATIC: | (A) sleepy | (B) essential | (C) empty |
| | (D) dissolved | (E) psychic | |

Part B

From the list below choose the word that best completes the analogy by expressing a relationship similar to that expressed in the original pair.

(A)	archaeology	(F)	felicity
(B)	adjunct	(G)	forte
(C)	acrimony	(H)	amorphous
(D)	celerity	(I)	pecuniary
(E)	definitive	(J)	therm

16. Judgment: adjudication:: conclusive: _____

17. Uniform: irregular:: weakness: _____

18. Services: honorarium:: wedding: _____

19. Words: etymology:: digging: _____

20. Athletics: sportsmanship:: marathon: _____

21. Purchase: monetary:: reward: _____

22. House: addition:: statement: _____

23. Electric: volt:: heat: _____

24. Anathema: curse:: formless: _____

25. Esoteric: manifest:: amiability: _____

Part C

From the list below select the words that best fit the meaning or context of the sentence.

(1)	atrophy	(5)	iconoclastic
(2)	audacious	(6)	reiterated
(3)	ectogenous	(7)	rejected
(4)	factitious		

26. A pilot fish maintains an _____ relationship with its host, the shark.

27. Although it started as a _____ smile, it ended as a real one.

28. Having _____ an appeal for a cease-fire, the Prime Minister _____ his refusal to pursue negotiations.

29. The _____ idea that the present view of the universe is wrong is an example of _____ thinking.

30. Often a patient's inactivity will cause his muscles to _____ and shrink.

Verbal Lesson Four

Simulated Verbal Examination

Time—30 Minutes

(The answers to the examination will be reviewed in televised Verbal Lesson Four or by your class-room teacher.)

Segment 1: Opposites

Select the word that is most nearly opposite in meaning to the word or phrase in capital letters. Consider any fine shades of meaning that may exist.

Example:

HOT: (A) green   (B) river   (C) cold
         (D) above   (E) sweet

	A	B	C	D	E
	○	○	●	○	○

1. PERNICIOUS: (A) liberal   (B) complimentary   (C) deciduous
                   (D) beneficial   (E) practical

2. ANTIPATHY: (A) guilt   (B) fondness   (C) secretiveness
                   (D) drama   (E) seniority

3. BENEFICENT: (A) great   (B) wasteful   (C) interfering
                   (D) indecisive   (E) miserly

4. RANCOR: (A) forgiveness   (B) mildness   (C) shame
                   (D) evaluator   (E) wits

5. AVARICE: (A) lummox   (B) message   (C) generosity
                   (D) chance   (E) preconception

6. NOXIOUS: (A) mediatory   (B) special   (C) original
                   (D) harmless   (E) cautious

7. MACHINATION: (A) orderliness   (B) forthrightness   (C) gesture
                   (D) declaration   (E) novelty

8. QUERULOUS: (A) poignant   (B) selfish   (C) sufficient
                   (D) composed   (E) popular

9. APOTHEOSIS: (A) debasement   (B) fruition   (C) substitution
                   (D) excellence   (E) ostracism

10. LACHRYMOSE: (A) noted   (B) self-conscious   (C) perceptive
                    (D) original   (E) cheerful

Segment 2: Sentence Completion

The blanks in each sentence indicate omitted words. Select the word or words that best fit the meaning of the entire sentence and should be inserted in the blank.

Example:

On a small farm in an arid climate one should not grow crops that need considerable _____

or _____ to ripen.

(A) fertilizer — attention   (B) space — water
(C) sun — air   (D) tilling — harvesting
(E) weeding — insecticides

A   B   C   D   E
○   ●   ○   ○   ○

---

11. As his annoyance increased, his speech became more _____.

   (A) conciliatory   (B) irate
   (C) cautious   (D) convincing
   (E) prudent

12. There is considerable _____ between the world as it is and the world as men perceive it.

   (A) resemblance   (B) symmetry
   (C) redundancy   (D) instability
   (E) divergence

13. Although we may appear quite dissimilar to different persons, we cling to the _____ that we

remain _____ for all.

   (A) myth — agreeable   (B) theory — enduring
   (C) supposition — changed   (D) illusion — identical
   (E) feeling — unique

14. His vindictiveness caused him to search for _____ instead of realistic proposals for _____.

   (A) explanations — quick solutions   (B) strategies — avoiding bloodshed
   (C) adversaries — mutual forgiveness   (D) causes — covering up
   (E) scapegoats — positive action

15. Mr. Butler's indignation was heightened by the _____ of his competitor whose _____

dealings ostensibly appeared fair and open.

   (A) duplicity — insidious   (B) zeal — conservative
   (C) shrewdness — innovative   (D) humility — corrupt
   (E) success — opportune

Segment 3: Analogies

Each question below contains a related pair of words or phrases followed by five lettered pairs of words or phrases. Select the answer that best expresses a relationship similar to that expressed in the original pair.

Example:

PURSUE: CATCH::

(A) occur: happen   (B) eat: drink
(C) track: overtake   (D) apprehend: chase
(E) contest: victory

A   B   C   D   E
○   ○   ●   ○   ○

---

16. COMMANDANT: FORT::

   (A) supervisor: accountability   (B) quarterback: pitcher
   (C) commissioner: government bureau   (D) communist: political party
   (E) doctor: hospital

17. SNIFF: NOSE::

   (A) sizzle: steak   (B) smack: lips
   (C) smell: odor   (D) shiver: cold
   (E) crack: nail

18. UNTIE: FREEDOM::

   (A) Houdini: chain   (B) inhibit: shyness
   (C) impound: confinement   (D) impute: honesty
   (E) minimize: value

19. GABBY: LOQUACIOUS::

   (A) talkative: words   (B) scold: bawl-out
   (C) hanky-panky: subterfuge   (D) surrender: capitulate
   (E) tough: scrawny

20. CATERPILLAR: BUTTERFLY::

   (A) teenager: grandmother   (B) seedling: redwood
   (C) twig: leaf   (D) cocoon: protection
   (E) tadpole: frog

21. ECSTATIC: GLAD::

   (A) curious: inquisitive   (B) discourteous: impolite
   (C) elated: pleased   (D) delighted: anguished
   (E) funny: laughable

22. UNANIMITY: DISCORD::

   (A) preventive: medicine   (B) prodigious: meager
   (C) gangster: crime   (D) tremble: earthquake
   (E) fabric: tapestry

23. PUNGENT: TONGUE::

   (A) combed: hair   (B) piercing: ear
   (C) looking: eye   (D) scented: nose
   (E) ruddy: cheek

24. CELIBATE: UNWEDDED::

   (A) widow: aged   (B) epicure: hedonistic
   (C) bridegroom: flirtatious   (D) benefactor: patriotic
   (E) polygamist: divorced

25. OPPOSE: RESIST::

(A) perform: accept
(B) differ: acquiesce
(C) unite: fuse
(D) certify: document
(E) assail: guard

Segment 4: Reading Comprehension

The questions following each passage are based on its content. Your choice should be made on the basis of what is stated *or implied in the passage.*

I once thought, when sailing up the Ohio one bright Northern summer, that the world held nothing more beautiful than the scenery of the Beautiful River—those voluptuous hills
5 with their sweet feminine curves, the elfin gold of that summer haze, and the pale emerald of the river's verdure-reflecting breast. But even the loveliness of the Ohio seemed faded, and the Northern sky-blue
10 palely cold, like the tint of iceberg pinnacles, when I beheld for the first time the splendor of the Mississippi.

"You must come on deck early tomorrow," said the kind Captain of the *Thompson Dean,*
15 "we are entering the Sugar Country."

So I saw the sun rise over the cane fields of Louisiana.

It rose with a splendor that recalled the manner of its setting at Memphis, but of
20 another color—an auroral flush of a pale gold and pale green bloomed over the long fringe of cottonwood and cypress trees, and broadened and lengthened halfway round the brightening world. The glow seemed tropical,
25 with the deep green of the trees sharply cutting against it; and one naturally looked for the feathery crests of coconut palms. Then the day broke gently and slowly—a day too vast for a rapid dawn—a day that seemed
30 deep as Space. I thought our Northern sky narrow and cramped as a vaulted church-roof beside that sky—a sky so softly beautiful, so purely clear in its immensity, that it made one dream of the tenderness of a woman's
35 eyes made infinite.

And the giant river broadened to a mile—smooth as a mirror, still and profound as a mountain lake. Between the vastness of the sky and the vastness of the stream, we seemed
40 moving suspended in the midst of day, with only a long, narrow tongue of land on either side breaking the brightness. Yet the horizon never became wholly blue. The green-golden glow lived there all through the day; it was
45 brightest in the South. It was so tropical,

that glow—it seemed of the Pacific, a glow
that forms a background to the sight of
lagoons and coral reefs and "lands where it
is always afternoon."
(Lafcadio Hearn, *Memphis to New Orleans*)

26. According to the passage, we can infer that

    (A)   The author is a travel agent
    (B)   The author is mapping river banks
    (C)   The author's destination is Memphis
    (D)   The author is traveling in a southerly direction
    (E)   The author prefers the scenery of the Ohio River to that of the Mississippi River

27. Which of the following statements best describes the passage?

    (A)   The author assumes the point of view of a biologist
    (B)   The author creates his impressions by relying on colorful images
    (C)   The author writes from an impersonal point of view
    (D)   The author employs sarcasm as a literary device
    (E)   The author is an experienced river pilot

28. According to the passage, the author compares the beauty of the Mississippi River to the beauty of

    (A)   Tropical Pacific islands
    (B)   A sunrise
    (C)   Memphis
    (D)   The South
    (E)   The North

29. According to the passage, the author

    (A)   Describes the last trip he will ever take down the Mississippi
    (B)   Describes the last trip he will ever take down the Ohio River
    (C)   Describes his first river-boat journey down the Mississippi River
    (D)   Describes a walking tour along the banks of the Mississippi and Ohio Rivers
    (E)   Describes a walking tour of the Ohio River and a river-boat journey on the Mississippi River

30. In the opening paragraph the author uses figurative language to compare the Ohio River to

    (A)   A river boat   (B) A winter sky
    (C)   Cypress trees   (D) A Greek goddess
    (E)   A woman

It was characteristic of Faraday's devotion
to the enlargements of the bounds of human
knowledge that on his discovery of magneto-
electricity he abandoned the commercial work
5 by which he had added to his small salary,
in order to reserve all his energies for research. This financial loss was in part made
up later by a pension of 300 pounds a year
from the British government.

10   Faraday's parents were members of the
obscure religious denomination of the Sande-
manians, and Faraday himself, shortly after
his marriage, at the age of thirty, joined the
same sect, to which he adhered till his death.
15 Religion and science he kept strictly apart,
believing that the data of science were of an

entirely different nature from the direct communications between God and the soul on which his religious faith was based.

20   The discoveries made by Faraday were so numerous, and often demand so detailed a knowledge of chemistry and physics before they can be understood, that it is impossible to attempt to describe or even enumerate
25   them here. Among the most important are the discovery of magneto-electric induction, of the law of electro-chemical decomposition, of the magnetization of light, and of diamagnetism. Each of these are highly important
30   additions to scientific knowledge, and together they form so vast an achievement as to lead his successor, Tyndall, to say, "Taking him for all and all, I think it will be conceded that Michael Faraday was the greatest experi-
35   mental philosopher the world has ever seen; and I will add the opinion, that the progress of future research will tend, not to dim or diminish, but to enhance and glorify the labours of this mighty investigator."

40   In spite of the highly technical nature of his work in research, Faraday was remarkably gifted as an expounder of science to popular audiences; and his lectures at the Royal Institution, especially those to younger audi-
45   ences, were justly famous.
(Charles W. Eliot, ed., *Harvard Classics: Scientific Papers*)

31. All of the following discoveries by Faraday are mentioned in the passage except
    (A)   Electro-magnetic adhesion   (B)   Magnetization of light
    (C)   Diamagnetism   (D)   Magneto-electric induction
    (E)   Electro-chemical decomposition

32. We can infer from the information in the passage that
    (A)   Before joining the Sandemanian sect, Faraday was an agnostic
    (B)   Faraday's salary from the British government was inadequate
    (C)   Tyndall played a significant role in the discoveries attributed to Faraday
    (D)   Faraday had the ability to explain highly technical material in simple, popular terms
    (E)   Faraday's discoveries came in fairly rapid succession

33. According to the passage, Faraday did not allow his religious beliefs and scientific studies to commingle because
    (A)   As a member of the Sandemanian sect he was not allowed to practice scientific experiments
    (B)   He believed that scientific knowledge was of a different nature than religious revelation
    (C)   As a scientist, he rejected religious dogma
    (D)   Physical and chemical laws disproved the existence of a divine being
    (E)   As an experimental philosopher, he was afraid that his discoveries would diminish his religious fervor

34. According to the passage, Faraday discontinued his commercial work because
    (A)   He wanted to devote all his time to research

(B)   It was not profitable
(C)   It conflicted with his religious beliefs
(D)   He was unsuccessful in commercial work
(E)   It conflicted with the work of his assistant, Tyndall

35. We can infer that Faraday's discoveries would have interest especially for

(A)   High school science students
(B)   Chemists and physicists
(C)   The average citizen
(D)   British schoolchildren
(E)   Laboratory assistants

But the object that most drew my attention, in the mysterious package, was a certain affair of fine red cloth, much worn and faded. There were traces about it of gold embroidery, which,
5 however, was greatly frayed and defaced; so that none, or very little, of the glitter was left. It had been wrought, as was easy to perceive, with wonderful skill of needlework; and the stitch (as I am assured by ladies conversant
10 with such mysteries) gives evidence of a now forgotten art, not to be recovered even by the process of picking out the threads. This rag of scarlet cloth—for time and wear and a sacrilegious moth had reduced it to little other
15 than a rag—on careful examination, assumed the shape of a letter. It was the capital letter A. By an accurate measurement, each limb proved to be precisely three inches and a quarter in length. It had been intended, there
20 could be no doubt, as an ornamental article of dress; but how it was to be worn, or what rank, honor, and dignity, in by-past times, were signified by it, was a riddle which (so evanescent are the fashions of the world in
25 these particulars) I saw little hope of solving. And yet it strangely interested me. My eyes fastened themselves upon the old scarlet letter, and would not be turned aside. Certainly, there was some deep meaning in it,
30 most worthy of interpretation, and which, as it were, streamed forth from the mystic symbol, subtly communicating itself to my sensibilities, but evading the analysis of my mind.

35 While thus perplexed—and cogitating, among other hypotheses, whether the letter might not have been one of those decorations which the white men used to contrive, in order to take the eyes of Indians—I happened to
40 place it on my breast. It seemed to me— the reader may smile, but must not doubt my word—it seemed to me, then, that I experienced a sensation not altogether physical, yet almost so, as of burning heat; and as if the
45 letter were not of red cloth, but red-hot iron.

I shuddered, and involuntarily let it fall upon
the floor.
(Nathaniel Hawthorne, *The Scarlet Letter*)

36. Which of the following best summarizes the content of the passage?

    (A) A description of ancient, magical rituals
    (B) A description of the contents of a mysterious package
    (C) A description of different patterns of needlework
    (D) A description of a particularly intriguing item in a package
    (E) A description of the writer's reaction to physical torture

37. The writer's tone in the passage is best described as

    (A) Humorous   (B) Disheartened
    (C) Suspenseful   (D) Defiant
    (E) Philosophical

38. According to the passage, which of the following about the scarlet letter is <u>not</u> mentioned?

    (A) It must have been fashioned by one highly skilled in needlework
    (B) It may have been created by white men as a trinket to be given to Indians
    (C) It may have been a symbol with deeper meaning
    (D) It may have been used in an earlier time as an ornament of dress
    (E) It may have had mysterious chemical properties which, when placed on the skin, caused a
         burn

39. According to the passage, which of the following statements about the letter is <u>not</u> true?

    I.   It had an hypnotic effect on the observer
    II. It was discovered among other items in a mysterious package
    III. It was discovered in remarkably good condition
    IV. It was a magical symbol used in mysterious rituals

    (A) I and III only   (B) II and IV only
    (C) I and II only   (D) III and IV only
    (E) IV only

40. Which of the following phrases is <u>not</u> used by the writer in describing the letter?

    (A) "Sacrilegious decoration"   (B) "Scarlet cloth"
    (C) "Mystic symbol"   (D) "Gold embroidery"
    (E) "Ornamental article"

Skill Builder—Sentence Completion

*The blanks in each sentence indicate omitted words. Select the word or words that best fit the
meaning of the entire sentence and should be inserted in the blank. The answers will be reviewed in
televised Verbal Lesson Four or by your classroom teacher.*

Example:

On a small farm in an arid climate one should not grow crops that need considerable _____

or _____ to ripen.

(A) fertilizer — attention   (B) space — water
(C) sun — air   (D) tilling — harvesting
(E) weeding — insecticides

                                       A   B   C   D   E
                                       ○   ●   ○   ○   ○

1. The cavalry attacked with remarkable swiftness but was _____ by the enemy's superior defenses.

   (A) infuriated   (B) betrayed
   (C) repulsed   (D) distracted
   (E) undermined

2. The _____ that erupted as applicants pushed and shoved one another caused officials to summon police in order to restore order.

   (A) rivalry   (B) pensiveness
   (C) bickering   (D) vituperation
   (E) melee

3. Many novels that attempt to mirror the world are really _____ of the _____ that they represent.

   (A) expressions — mystery   (B) affirmations — principles
   (C) reflections — reality   (D) retractions — society
   (E) assessments — illusiveness

4. Many Americans seem to have forgotten the _____ that forced their ancestors to create a government _____ of oppressive powers.

   (A) evils — stripped   (B) principles — supportive
   (C) fears — protective   (D) abuses — independent
   (E) practices — tolerant

5. Even the most _____ scientists must recognize the realistic fear that atomic energy may become a weapon of universal destruction rather than a tool of planetary _____.

   (A) idealistic — contamination   (B) perceptive — strength
   (C) dogmatic — health   (D) praiseworthy — fighting
   (E) bellicose — extinction

Reading Comprehension

The questions following each passage are based on its content. Your choice should be made on the basis of what is stated or implied in the passage.

Exercise A—Narrative

As I walked home in a pensive mood, my vanity got the better of my pity. I could not but highly plume myself on my masterly management in getting rid of Bartleby.
5 Masterly I call it, and such it must appear to any dispassionate thinker. The beauty of my procedure seemed to consist in its perfect quietness. There was no vulgar bullying, no bravado of any sort, no
10 CHOLERIC HECTORING, and striding to and fro across the apartment, jerking out vehement commands for Bartleby to bundle himself off with his beggarly traps. Nothing of

the kind. Without loudly bidding Bartleby depart—as an inferior genius might have done—
I assumed the ground that depart he must;
and upon that assumption built all I have to
say. The more I thought over my procedure,
the more I was charmed with it. Nevertheless,
next morning, upon awakening I had my
doubts—I had somehow slept off the fumes of
vanity. One of the coolest and wisest hours a
man has, is just after he awakes in the morning. My procedure seemed as sagacious as ever
—but only in theory. How it would prove in
practice—there was the rub. It was truly a
beautiful thought to have assumed Bartleby's
departure; but, after all, that assumption was
simply my own, and none of Bartleby's. The
great point was, not whether I had assumed
that he would quit me, but whether he would
prefer so to do. He was more a man of pref-
erences than assumptions.

After breakfast, I walked downtown, arguing
the probabilities pro and con. One moment
I thought it would prove a miserable failure,
and Bartleby would be found all alive at my
office as usual; the next moment it seemed
certain that I should find his chair empty.
And so I kept veering about. At the corner of
Broadway and Canal Street, I saw quite an
excited group of people standing in earnest
conversation.

"I'll take odds he doesn't," said a voice as
I passed.

"Doesn't go?—done!" said I; "put up your
money."

I was instinctively putting my hand in my
pocket to produce my own, when I remem-
bered that this was an election day. The
words I had overheard bore no reference to
Bartleby, but to the success or non-success
of some candidate for the mayoralty. In my
intent frame of mind, I had, as it were, imag-
ined that all Broadway shared in my excitement, and were debating the same question
with me. I passed on, very thankful that the
uproar of the street screened my momentary
absentmindedness.

As I had intended, I was earlier than usual
at my office door. I stood listening for a
moment. All was still. He must be gone. I
tried the knob. The door was locked. Yes, my
procedure had worked to a charm; he indeed

91

65 must be vanished. Yet a certain melancholy
mixed with this: I was almost sorry for my
brilliant success. I was fumbling under the
door mat for the key, which Bartleby was to
have left there for me, when accidentally my
70 knee knocked against a panel, producing a
summoning sound, and in response a voice
came to me from within—"Not yet; I am
occupied."

It was Bartleby.
(Herman Melville, *Bartleby*)

6. According to the passage, while walking home

(A) The speaker refuses to allow himself to become emotionally upset regarding the earlier
    scene with Bartleby
(B) The speaker prides himself on the way he handled Bartleby
(C) The speaker chides himself for forgetting that it was election day
(D) The speaker convinces himself that Bartleby will arrive for work as usual the next day
(E) The speaker regrets the abusive language he used in his earlier conversation with
    Bartleby

7. It can be inferred from the passage that the relationship between the speaker and Bartleby is
one of

(A) Employee to employer   (B) Father to son
(C) Coworker to coworker   (D) Secretary to boss
(E) Employer to employee

8. The phrase CHOLERIC HECTORING as used in lines 9 and 10 means

(A) Indifferent complacency   (B) Genuine benevolence
(C) Heartfelt gratitude   (D) Bad-tempered intimidation
(E) Tender sympathy

9. According to the passage, the speaker believes that

(A) He was guilty of giving Bartleby too much independence
(B) He offended Bartleby's sensitive nature
(C) He used firm yet gentle arguments in dismissing Bartleby
(D) He offered Bartleby the opportunity to make his own choices
(E) He made too many demands upon Bartleby

10. The speaker's thoughts suggest that he is

(A) Confident yet forgetful   (B) Skeptical and aloof
(C) Compassionate and humble   (D) Pompous and scholarly
(E) Vain yet doubting

Vocabulary Builder

Follow the instructions for each of the exercises. Answer keys are provided at the end of the vocabulary builder section. Before doing the exercises, familiarize *yourself with the* 10 Key Prefixes, 11 Important Roots, *the* Greek and Latin Numerals, *the* Scientific Terminology, *and the* Essential Words.

10 Key Prefixes

1. ante... *before, previous in time, prior to* (Lat.)

2. apo... *off, from, away from* (Gr.)

3. contra .... *opposite, against* (Lat.)

4. hyper .... *over, above, excessive* (Gr.)

5. hypo .... *under* (Gr.)

6. intro, intra .... *within, into, inward* (Lat.)

7. mal(e) .... *evil, bad, ill, wrong* (Lat.)

8. meta .... *between, with, after* (Gr.)

9. micro .... *small, little* (Gr.)

10. per[1] .... *through, thoroughly* (Lat.)

1. *per* conveys six meanings: (1) through (percolate); (2) throughout, to the end (perennial, perorate); (3) thoroughly, completely (perfect, perceive); (4) away (perdition, peregrine); (5) destruction (perfidy, perjure); (6) intensified action (perform).

11 Important Roots

1. grat .... *pleasing, grateful* (Lat.)

2. luc, lux, lumen .... *light, shining* (Lat.)

3. mort, mori .... *death, die* (Lat.)

4. nomen, nomin .... *name* (Lat.)

5. pend, pens, pond .... *hang, weigh, pay* (Lat.)

6. plac .... *please, appease* (Lat.)

7. plen, ple(t) .... *full, fill* (Lat.)

8. prol .... *offspring* (Lat.)

9. purg .... *clean* (Lat.)

10. sat .... *enough* (Lat.)

11. viv, vita, vict .... *live, life* (Lat.)

14 Greek and 14 Latin Numerals
Greek

MON(O)	meaning *one* as in *monotone*
DI	meaning *twice, double* as in *dioxide*
DICH	meaning *in two* as in *dichotomy*
DEUTER	meaning *second* as in *deuterogamy*
TRI	meaning *three* as in *triad*
TETR(A)	meaning *four* as in *tetrapod*
PENT(A)	meaning *five* as in *pentagon*
HEX(A)	meaning *six* as in *hexagram*
HEPT(A)	meaning *seven* as in *heptameter*
OCT(A)	meaning *eight* as in *octopus*
DEC(A)	meaning *ten* as in *decathlon*
HECT	meaning *a hundred* as in *hectometer*
KILO	meaning *a thousand* as in *kilogram*
HEMI	meaning *half* as in *hemisphere*

ENNEA meaning *nine* is used infrequently

Latin

UN	meaning *one* as in *unanimous*
PRIM	meaning *first* as in *primitive*
DU	meaning *two* as in *dual*
BI, BIN	meaning *two, twice* as in *binoculars*
TRI	meaning *three* as in *triangle*
QUADR	meaning *four* as in *quadruple*
QUART	meaning *fourth* as in *quarter*
SEXT	meaning *six* as in *sextet*
SEPT, SEPTEM	meaning *seven* as in *septet*
OCT	meaning *eight* as in *octet*
DECI, DECIM	meaning *tenth* as in *decimal*
CENT	meaning *hundred* as in *centennial*
MILL	meaning *thousand* as in *millimeter*
SEMI	meaning *half* as in *semiannual*

TERTI *(third)* and NOVEM *(ninth)* are used infrequently

Scientific Terminology from Greek Roots

1. aden: *gland* as in *adenoid*
2. arthr: *joint* as in *arthritis*
3. carcin: *crab* as in *carcinogen, carcinoma*
4. cardi: *heart* as in *cardiac*
5. chol: *bile; gall* as in *cholesterol*
6. cyt: *cell* as in *cytology*
7. hemat (hemo): *blood* as in *hemorrhage, hemophilia*
8. hepat: *liver* as in *hepatitis*
9. hypn: *sleep* as in *hypnotic*
10. melan: *black, dark* as in *melanoma, melange*
11. nephr: *kidney* as in *nephrosis*
12. neur: *nerve* as in *neural, neuralgia*
13. oste: *bone* as in *osteopathy, osteology*

Essential Words—Human Relations

1. Bravado—*(N)* boasting; swaggering
2. Capricious—*(Adj)* governed or characterized by caprice; apt to change suddenly; fickle
3. Cynic—*(N)* one who sarcastically doubts human motives
4. Dispassionate—*(Adj)* impartial; calm
5. Maudlin—*(Adj)* weakly sentimental
6. Narcissism—*(N)* abnormal attachment to one's own appearance and personality
7. Obsequious—*(Adj)* slavishly attentive; cringing; fawning
8. Pensive—*(Adj)* gravely thoughtful
9. Puerile—*(Adj)* childish
10. Pugnacious—*(Adj)* fond of fighting
11. Recalcitrant—*(Adj)* resisting control
12. Sagacious—*(Adj)* keen in sensing; quick and shrewd in understanding and judging; discerning
13. Solicitous—*(Adj)* anxious; concerned
14. Stoic—*(Adj)* impassive; indifferent to pleasure or pain
15. Sycophant—*(N)* flatterer; parasite

Essential Words—World of Practical Affairs

1. Aegis—*(N)* sponsorship
2. Draconian—*(N)* extremely severe
3. Ensconce—*(V)* to shelter or hide; to settle comfortably
4. Expound—*(V)* state in detail
5. Fiduciary—*(Adj)* being a trustee; held in trust
6. Fraternal—*(Adj)* brotherly
7. Hiatus—*(N)* an opening; gap—esp. a break with a part missing
8. Indemnity—*(N)* protection from loss or damage; insurance
9. Matriarchy—*(N)* a family, group, or state ruled by a woman
10. Ostracism—*(N)* exclusion from society
11. Sect—*(N)* group with a common religious faith
12. Sequester—*(V)* to set apart; separate; segregate—to remove from public view
13. Solecism—*(N)* a substandard usage of language; a social blunder
14. Sophistry—*(N)* clever but unsound reasoning
15. Surreptitious—*(Adj)* stealth; secret

Essential Words—Aesthetic-Philosophical

1. Abstruse—*(Adj)* hard to understand
2. Aeolian—*(Adj)* produced by the wind
3. Arcadian—*(Adj)* simple, peaceful, rustic
4. Chimera—*(N)* a foolish or idle fancy
5. Elysium—*(N)* place or state of blissful happiness
6. Epicure—*(N)* a person of refined taste in food and drink
7. Halcyon—*(Adj)* calm, peaceful
8. Moot—*(Adj)* debatable
9. Nemesis—*(N)* retribution
10. Perspicuous—*(Adj)* clear to the understanding
11. Stentorian—*(Adj)* very loud
12. Tantalize—*(V)* torment by sight of something desired; tease
13. Titanic—*(Adj)* of enormous size and power
14. Ubiquitous—*(Adj)* present everywhere at the same time
15. Voluptuous—*(Adj)* luxurious; sensuous

Essential Words—Science Related

1. Aural—*(Adj)* pertaining to the ear
2. Choleric—*(Adj)** prone to anger
3. Derivative—*(N)* anything derived from some other thing
4. Dichotomy—*(N)* division into two subordinate parts
5. Hybrid—*(N)* the offspring of two animals or plants of different species
6. Induction—*(N)* reasoning from particular facts
7. Labyrinth—*(N)* maze—a complicated series of passageways
8. Mandible—*(N)* jaw
9. Obelisk—*(N)* tapering four-sided stone
10. Orifice—*(N)* opening
11. Periphery—*(N)* external boundary or surface

*It was once thought that bile made a person angry.

12. Pinnacle—*(N)* lofty peak or position—top
13. Precipice—*(N)* a sharp cliff
14. Protean—*(Adj)* extremely changeable
15. Suture—*(N)* stitch used to close a wound

Exercise 1—Roots

Match the Root in Column A with its meaning in Column B.

Column A

1. cardi
2. chol
3. cyt
4. grat
5. luc, lux, lumen
6. melan
7. mort, mori
8. nephr
9. nomen, nomin
10. pend, pens, pond
11. plac
12. plen, ple(t)
13. prol
14. purg
15. sat
16. viv, vita, vict

Column B

(A) hang, weigh, pay
(B) bile; gall
(C) name
(D) full, fill
(E) clean
(F) cell
(G) enough
(H) please, appease
(I) offspring
(J) kidney
(K) live, life
(L) heart
(M) death, die
(N) light, shining
(O) pleasing, grateful
(P) black

1. _____ 5. _____ 9. _____ 13. _____

2. _____ 6. _____ 10. _____ 14. _____

3. _____ 7. _____ 11. _____ 15. _____

4. _____ 8. _____ 12. _____ 16. _____

Exercise 2—Prefixes and Numerical Elements

Match the Prefix or the Numerical Element in Column A with its meaning in Column B.

Column A

1. ante
2. apo
3. contra
4. decim, deci
5. intro, intra
6. hemi
7. hyper
8. hypo
9. mal(e)
10. meta
11. micro
12. mon(o)
13. per
14. prim
15. semi
16. sept, septem

Column B

(A) through, thoroughly;
(B) evil, bad, ill, wrong
(C) before, previous in time, prior to
(D) between, with, after
(E) one
(F) over, above, excessive
(G) off, from, away from
(H) tenth
(I) within, into, inward
(J) seven
(K) opposite, against
(L) half
(M) under
(N) first
(O) small, little
(P) half, partly

1. _____	5. _____	9. _____	13. _____
2. _____	6. _____	10. _____	14. _____
3. _____	7. _____	11. _____	15. _____
4. _____	8. _____	12. _____	16. _____

Exercise 3

For each of the key words in Exercise 3 select from the list below one word that is most nearly the same in meaning to the key word and one word that is most nearly opposite to the key word. The first one is done for you.

Synonyms	Antonyms
1. abundance	acceptance
2. acme	annual
3. ancient	appreciable
4. atrophy	benevolent
5. banishment	compliant
6. belligerent	dark
7. dominant	deprive
8. gorge	devitalize
9. gratification	discontent
10. imperceptible	dull
11. lucid	expansion
12. malicious	extroverted
13. melancholy	ignorant
14. obstinate	insignificant
15. perpetual	invigorate
16. previous	modern
17. purify	nadir
18. radiant	pacific
19. reproduce	pollute
20. roaring	satisfy
21. shrewd	scarcity
22. summary	subdued
23. tease	subsequent
24. wise	thoughtless
25. withdrawn	turbid

---

1. Antecedent
KEY WORD

ante	ced	ent
prefix(es)	root	suffix(es)

to go before	a previous thing or event; something happening before and leading up to another
literal meaning	definition

previous	subsequent
synonym	antonym

97

2. Antediluvian
KEY WORD

ante	diluvium	
prefix(es)	root	suffix(es)

before the deluge	belonging to times before the Flood; very old or old-fashioned
literal meaning	definition

synonym	antonym

3. Compendium
KEY WORD

com	pend	ium
prefix(es)	root	suffix(es)

that which is weighed together	a short, complete summary
literal meaning	definition

synonym	antonym

4. Devitalize
KEY WORD

de	vita	ize
prefix(es)	root	suffix(es)

reverse the life of	to destroy the vitality of
literal meaning	definition

synonym	antonym

5. Imponderable
KEY WORD

im	pond(er)	able
prefix(es)	root	suffix(es)

not able to be weighed	incapable of being weighed or measured with preciseness
literal meaning	definition

synonym	antonym

6. Introverted
KEY WORD

intro	vert	
prefix(es)	root	suffix(es)

to turn inward

literal meaning

to concentrate (one's interests) upon oneself; a person whose thoughts or interests are directed inward

definition

synonym   antonym

7. Luminous
KEY WORD

	lumin	ous
prefix(es)	root	suffix(es)

having to do with light

literal meaning

radiating or emitting light; clear; lucid

definition

synonym   antonym

8. Malevolent
KEY WORD

male	volent (stem of volens)	
prefix(es)	root	suffix(es)

wishing evil

literal meaning

having or exhibiting ill-will; wishing harm to others

definition

synonym   antonym

9. Ostracism
KEY WORD

	ostra(c)	ism
prefix(es)	root	suffix(es)

shell, shard (with which Athenian citizens voted for ostracism)

literal meaning

exclusion from a group; disgrace

definition

synonym   antonym

10. Pensive
KEY WORD

prefix(es)	pens root	ive suffix(es)

having to do with weighing (thinking) literal meaning	thoughtful in a serious or sad way definition

synonym	antonym

11. Perennial
KEY WORD

per prefix(es)	enn (a form of annus: year) root	al suffix(es)

through the year literal meaning	lasting through a whole year; lasting a long time; enduring definition

synonym	antonym

12. Perspicacious
KEY WORD

CAUTION: Do not confuse Perspicacious with Perspicuous

per prefix(es)	[spic (spec)] (aci) root	ous suffix(es)

to look through literal meaning	keen in observing and understanding; discerning definition

synonym	antonym

13. Perspicuous
KEY WORD

CAUTION: Do not confuse Perspicuous with Perspicacious

per prefix(es)	[spic (spec)] (u) root	ous suffix(es)

to see through literal meaning	clearly expressed or presented definition

synonym	antonym

14. Pertinacious
KEY WORD

per	ten(aci)	ous
prefix(es)	root	suffix(es)

to hold thoroughly	holding firmly or tenaciously to some purpose or opinion
literal meaning	definition

synonym	antonym

15. Pinnacle
KEY WORD

	pinna	cle
prefix(es)	root	suffix(es)

wing	the highest point
literal meaning	definition

synonym	antonym

16. Plenitude
KEY WORD

	plen(i)	tude
prefix(es)	root	suffix(es)

full	the condition of being full, ample, complete
literal meaning	definition

synonym	antonym

17. Preponderant
KEY WORD

pre	pond(er)	ant
prefix(es)	root	suffix(es)

to weigh before	greater in amount, weight, power, influence, etc.
literal meaning	definition

synonym	antonym

18. Proliferate
KEY WORD

prefix(es)	prol(ifer)	ate
	root	suffix(es)

producing offspring	to reproduce or produce new growth or parts rapidly; to spread at a rapid rate
literal meaning	definition

synonym	antonym

19. Pugnacious
KEY WORD

prefix(es)	pugn(aci)	ous
	root	suffix(es)

fond of fighting	eager and ready to fight
literal meaning	definition

synonym	antonym

20. Purge
KEY WORD

prefix(es)	purg	suffix(es)
	root	

to cleanse	to rid of whatever is impure or undesirable; to atone (for an offense)
literal meaning	definition

synonym	antonym

21. Sagacious
KEY WORD

prefix(es)	sag(aci)	ous
	root	suffix(es)

to perceive acutely	wise in a keen, practical way; intelligent
literal meaning	definition

synonym	antonym

22. Satiate
KEY WORD

prefix(es)	sat(i)	ate
	root	suffix(es)

having enough	feed fully; satisfy fully; weary with too much
literal meaning	definition

synonym	antonym

23. Satisfaction
KEY WORD

prefix(es)	satis/fact	ion
	root	suffix(es)

doing enough	fulfillment of conditions or desires; pleased
literal meaning	definition

synonym	antonym

24. Stentorian
KEY WORD

prefix(es)	stentor	ian
	root	suffix(es)

loud-voiced herald in the Iliad	having a very loud voice
literal meaning	definition

synonym	antonym

25. Tantalize
KEY WORD

prefix(es)	tantal	ize
	root	suffix(es)

son of Zeus (Myth)	to tease or disappoint by showing something desirable and then withholding it
literal meaning	definition

synonym	antonym

Exercise 4—Root Words and Meanings

Fill in the blanks with the correct words.

1. The root _____ is found in *devitalize*.

   DEVITALIZE means _____ .

2. The root _____ is found in *elucidate*.

   ELUCIDATE means _____ .

3. The root _____ is found in *gratified*.

   GRATIFIED means _____ .

4. The root _____ is found in *ignominious*.

   IGNOMINIOUS means _____ .

5. The root _____ is found in *moribund*.

   MORIBUND means _____ .

6. The root _____ is found in *placate*.

   PLACATE means _____ .

7. The root _____ is found in *plenitude*.

   PLENITUDE means _____ .

8. The root _____ is found in *proletariat*.

   PROLETARIAT means _____ .

9. The root _____ is found in *purgative*.

   PURGATIVE means _____ .

10. The root _____ is found in *satiate*.

   SATIATE means _____ .

Exercise 5—Essential Words

Match each word in Column A with its definition in Column B.

Column A		Column B	
1.	abstruse	(A)	opening
2.	arcadian	(B)	clever but unsound reasoning
3.	choleric	(C)	resisting control
4.	fraternal	(D)	exclusion from society
5.	moot	(E)	brotherly
6.	orifice	(F)	hard to understand
7.	ostracism	(G)	debatable
8.	pugnacious	(H)	prone to anger
9.	recalcitrant	(I)	simple, peaceful, rustic
10.	sophistry	(J)	fond of fighting

1. _____   6. _____

2. _____   7. _____

3. _____   8. _____

4. _____   9. _____

5. _____   10. _____

Exercise 6—Antonyms

Match each word in Column A with the word most nearly opposite in Column B.

Column A

1. chimera
2. choleric
3. cynic
4. periphery
5. puerile
6. pugnacious
7. solicitous
8. stentorian
9. tantalize
10. titanic

Column B

(A) reality
(B) miniature
(C) mild-mannered
(D) interior
(E) satisfy
(F) uncaring
(G) quiet
(H) pacifying
(I) optimist
(J) mature

1. _____   6. _____

2. _____   7. _____

3. _____   8. _____

4. _____   9. _____

5. _____   10. _____

Exercise 7—Sentence Completion

Complete the sentences in Column B by filling in the blank with the correct word from Column A.

Column A

1. capricious

2. chimera

3. ensconced

4. fiduciary

5. maudlin

6. obsequious

7. pinnacle

Column B

1. We were _____ in the basement during the hurricane.

2. The shy old man _____ himself from all strangers.

3. The famous rock music star was at the _____ of his career.

4. Her _____ nature caused her to become bored very quickly.

5. A guardian acts in a _____ capacity.

6. We watched a _____ television show about a child and a dog.

7. A mother is _____ about her child's progress in school.

105

8. sequestered

8. _____ courtiers greeted the King and Queen.

9. solicitous

9. The hope of changing dirt to gold was a _____.

10. stentorian

10. The drill sergeant shouted the command in a _____ voice.

Vocabulary Check Test

(Answers will be reviewed in televised Verbal Lesson Four or by your classroom teacher.)

Part A

Choose the word or phrase most nearly opposite to the word in capital letters.

1. APOSTATE:
   - (A) impostor
   - (B) troublemaker
   - (C) devotee
   - (D) deserter
   - (E) mendicant

2. CHIMERICAL:
   - (A) embarrassed
   - (B) feasible
   - (C) ringing
   - (D) incessant
   - (E) perishable

3. CATASTROPHE:
   - (A) punctuation
   - (B) chronicle
   - (C) abomination
   - (D) intrusion
   - (E) blessing

4. PLENARY:
   - (A) limited
   - (B) fiscal
   - (C) feast
   - (D) peculiar
   - (E) forgiving

5. LUCID:
   - (A) evil
   - (B) confused
   - (C) careful
   - (D) fatal
   - (E) glossy

6. PURGE:
   - (A) pollute
   - (B) lie
   - (C) perforate
   - (D) seclude
   - (E) sermonize

7. EPICUREAN:
   - (A) yearly
   - (B) gigantic
   - (C) self-denying
   - (D) exaggerated
   - (E) sober

8. SATIATE:
   - (A) fatigue
   - (B) deprive
   - (C) quench
   - (D) moisten
   - (E) covet

9. MELANCHOLY:
   - (A) ephemeral
   - (B) facetious
   - (C) fictitious
   - (D) dreadful
   - (E) jolly

10. PSYCHOGENIC:
    - (A) physical
    - (B) demented
    - (C) supernatural
    - (D) inherited
    - (E) intuitive

11. GRATIFICATION:
    - (A) ignorance
    - (B) behavior
    - (C) disappointment
    - (D) sensitivity
    - (E) veto

12. TANTALIZE:
    - (A) brainwash
    - (B) equalize
    - (C) indulge
    - (D) satisfy
    - (E) corrugate

13. HOMOGENEOUS:
    - (A) dissimilar
    - (B) wanton
    - (C) analytical
    - (D) mythical
    - (E) precocious

14. ENIGMATIC:
    - (A) sloppy
    - (B) regretful
    - (C) agreeable
    - (D) exciting
    - (E) self-evident

15. GERMANE:
    - (A) disillusioned
    - (B) pleasurable
    - (C) profitable
    - (D) extraneous
    - (E) cautious

Part B

From the list below choose the word that best completes the analogy by expressing a relationship similar to that expressed in the original pair.

(A) apogee
(B) arcadian
(C) ignominy
(D) mentor
(E) monogamist

(F) moribundity
(G) octave
(H) orthopedics
(I) paradox
(J) plenitude

16. Close: distant:: perigee: _____

17. Locust: defoliation:: malfeasance: _____

18. Uniformity: incongruity:: paucity: _____

19. Right: franchise:: obsolescence: _____

20. Rural: sylvan:: rustic: _____

21. Heart attack: cardiology:: broken bone: _____

22. Representation: lawyer:: advice: _____

23. Obligation: duty:: contradiction: _____

24. Pentagon: quintet:: octopus: _____

25. Language: polyglot:: marriage: _____

Part C

From the list below select the two words that best fit the meaning or context of the sentence.

(1) elucidate
(2) invincible
(3) labyrinth
(4) lucidity
(5) odyssey

(6) protean
(7) soliloquy
(8) stentorian
(9) translucent
(10) vociferous

26. To throw more light on the subject, the English professor attempted to _____ a difficult _____ from Shakespeare's *Hamlet*.

27. The _____ nature of his character revealed itself when suddenly a whisper became a _____ roar.

28. The fog suddenly became more _____, and with corresponding _____ he realized his precarious situation.

29. With _____ tenacity he continued his _____ outcries against injustice.

30. In the course of our wanderings our _____ took us through a _____ of streets so that we soon lost all idea of where we were.

Verbal
Lesson
Five

Simulated Verbal Examination

Time—30 Minutes

(The answers to the examination will be reviewed in televised Verbal Lesson Five or by your classroom teacher.)

Segment 1: Opposites

Select the word that is most nearly opposite in meaning to the word or phrase in capital letters. Consider any fine shades of meaning that may exist.

Example:

HOT: (A) green   (B) river   (C) cold
        (D) above   (E) sweet

```
              A    B    C    D    E
              ○    ○    ●    ○    ○
```

1. ABOMINABLE: (A) controversial   (B) enigmatic   (C) final
                      (D) lovable   (E) noticeable

2. GUILE: (A) candor   (B) suggestion   (C) costume
                      (D) gesture   (E) blame

3. REPUDIATE: (A) acknowledge   (B) sacrifice   (C) search
                      (D) obstruct   (E) belittle

4. ZEPHYR: (A) young animal   (B) fabric   (C) cave
                      (D) despair   (E) gale

5. REPUGNANT: (A) ugly   (B) congenial   (C) tamable
                      (D) belligerent   (E) recurrent

6. LAUDABLE: (A) irksome   (B) loud   (C) blamable
                      (D) lively   (E) eccentric

7. RAPACIOUS: (A) active   (B) creative   (C) magnetic
                      (D) angry   (E) generous

8. PUNCTILIOUS: (A) careless   (B) scrupulous   (C) sweet
                      (D) fashionable   (E) impertinent

9. VERACITY: (A) strength (B) minority (C) elasticity
         (D) duplicity (E) agitation

10. PERSPICUITY: (A) incitement (B) ambiguity (C) obedience
         (D) purity   (E) debauchery

Segment 2: Sentence Completion

The blanks in each sentence indicate omitted words. Select the word or words that best *fit the meaning of the entire sentence and should be inserted in the blank.*

Example:

On a small farm in an arid climate one should not grow crops that need considerable _____

or _____ to ripen.

(A) fertilizer — attention   (B) space — water
(C) sun — air   (D) tilling — harvesting
(E) weeding — insecticides

                A B C D E
                ○ ● ○ ○ ○

11. A melody is a _____ of musical tones conveying an impression of _____: a series of pitches

arranged in logical sequence.

(A) separation — randomness   (B) balance — asymmetry
(C) performance — spontaneity   (D) succession — continuity
(E) recording — harmony

12. A discriminating listener always appreciates a _____ speaker instead of a _____ one.

(A) vital — credible   (B) succinct — verbose
(C) fallacious — pretentious   (D) conventional — predictable
(E) muffled — piercing

13. Anderson's failure to place nationalistic ideas into an historical context is _____ by his in-depth

analysis of the civil rights movement.

(A) substantiated   (B) contradicted
(C) compensated   (D) diminished
(E) augmented

14. Prohibition had the _____ effect of making alcohol more _____ to many Americans.

(A) desired — tempting   (B) limited — obtainable
(C) unexpected — legitimate   (D) paradoxical — attractive
(E) constitutional — manageable

15. Like an armed warrior he threw his _____ against the _____ of his country and the

maligners of his honor.

(A) shield — defilers   (B) lance — defamers
(C) body — critics   (D) javelin — champions
(E) banner — commanders

Segment 3: Analogies

Each question below contains a related pair of words or phrases followed by five lettered pairs of words or phrases. Select the answer that best expresses a relationship similar to that expressed in the original pair.

Example:

PURSUE: CATCH::

(A) occur: happen
(C) track: overtake
(E) contest: victory

(B) eat: drink
(D) apprehend: chase

A   B   C   D   E
○   ○   ●   ○   ○

---

16. ARSON: FIRE::

    (A) homicide: death
    (C) juvenile: delinquent
    (E) felony: transgression

    (B) thief: jewelry
    (D) robbery: house

17. PIER: WATER::

    (A) jetty: rocks
    (C) irrigation: ditch
    (E) ramp: car

    (B) vessel: boat
    (D) balcony: main floor

18. BRAY: DONKEYS::

    (A) leather: horses
    (C) den: lions
    (E) spawn: fishes

    (B) grass: cattle
    (D) grunt: hogs

19. SCENARIO: PLAY::

    (A) brevity: redundance
    (C) precis: book
    (E) locale: action

    (B) paint: design
    (D) acting: dialog

20. ENTOMOLOGY: INSECTS::

    (A) pathology: diseases
    (C) chronology: watches
    (E) ornithology: robins

    (B) meteorology: comets
    (D) demography: children

21. SOLILOQUY: DRAMA::

    (A) acting: performance
    (C) yodel: song
    (E) aria: opera

    (B) scene: stage
    (D) movement: melody

22. MAZE: DISORIENTATION::

    (A) spell: incantation
    (C) infatuation: obsession
    (E) web: entrapment

    (B) bandage: wound
    (D) opulence: diamonds

23. NOSTALGIA: PAST::

(A) punctuality: time
(C) radial: tire
(E) antiquity: Roman

(B) practice: football
(D) quixotic: question

24. CHARISMATIC: REPULSIVE::

(A) parallelism: homogeneity
(C) siren: bewitching
(E) banish: outcast

(B) glamorous: contemptible
(D) insolence: shameful

25. IMPUGN: ATTACK::

(A) stigmatize: mark
(C) remember: forget
(E) hesitate: act

(B) stifle: scold
(D) earn: spend

Segment 4: Reading Comprehension

The questions following each passage are based on its content. Your choice should be made on the basis of what is stated or implied in the passage.

If, then, we reduce the frog's nervous system to the spinal cord alone, by making a section behind the base of the skull, between the spinal cord and the medulla oblongata, there-
5 by cutting off the brain from all connection with the rest of the body, the frog will still continue to live, but with a very peculiarly modified activity. It ceases to breathe or swallow; it lies flat on its belly, and does
10 not, like a normal frog, sit up on its fore paws, though its hind legs are kept, as usual, folded against its body and immediately resume this position if drawn out. If thrown on its back, it lies there quietly, without turning over like
15 a normal frog. Locomotion and voice seem entirely abolished. If we irritate different portions of its skin, it performs a set of remarkable "defensive" movements. Thus, if the breast be touched, both fore paws will rub it
20 vigorously; if we touch the outer side of the elbow, the hind foot of the same side will rise directly to the spot and wipe it. The back of the foot will rub the knee if that be attacked.

25 The most striking character of all these movements, after their teleological* appropriateness, is their precision. They vary in sensitive frogs so little as almost to resemble in their machinelike regularity the perfor-
30 mances of a jumping-jack, whose legs must twitch whenever you pull the string. The spinal cord of the frog thus contains arrange-

Teleology is the belief that purpose and design are a part of nature.

111

ments of cells and fibres fitted to convert skin irritations into movements of defense. We may call it the center for defensive movements in this animal. We may indeed go farther than this, and by cutting the spinal cord in various places find that its separate segments are independent mechanisms, for appropriate activities of the head and of the arms and legs respectively. The segment governing the arms is especially active, in male frogs, in the breeding season; and these members alone with the breast and back appertaining to them, everything else being cut away, will then actively grasp a finger placed between them and remain hanging to it for a considerable time.

The spinal cord in other animals has analogous powers. Even in man it makes movements of defense.
(William James, *Principles of Psychology*)

26. The author's main purpose apparently is to

(A) Criticize present methods of dissecting frogs
(B) Evaluate the various physical movements of a frog after death
(C) Demonstrate the frog's spinal cord as the center for the animal's defensive movements
(D) Contrast the functions of a frog's brain and spinal cord
(E) Propose the correct manner of dissecting frogs

27. The author's tone suggests that his attitude toward the dissection of laboratory animals is one of

(A) Aloof disinterest
(B) Anxious concern
(C) Skeptical suspicion
(D) Scientific objectivity
(E) Casual interest

28. Based upon the author's contentions, we can conclude that

(A) A frog will die if a cut is made between its spinal cord and medulla oblongata
(B) Man's defensive movements are strictly controlled by his brain
(C) The brain plays no role in the frog's defensive actions against skin irritants
(D) A frog's movements will be erratic if its spinal cord is segmented
(E) The frog's nervous system is as complex as man's

29. According to the passage, if a cut is made between a frog's spinal cord and its medulla oblongata, which of the following statements is not true?

(A) It will stop normal breathing
(B) It will be unable to right itself if turned on its back
(C) Its hind legs will be folded, in normal position, against its body
(D) It will lose its voice
(E) It will use its fore paws and hind legs to sit upright

30. On the basis of the information in the passage, which of the following conclusions can be made?

I. A frog's spinal cord controls its reactions to skin irritants
II. The spinal cords of man and animal differ
III. A frog's brain transmits sensations to its spinal cord

(A) I only   (B) II only
(C) III only   (D) I and III only
(E) I, II, and III

        Though society is not founded on a contract, and though no good purpose is answered by inventing a contract in order to deduce social obligations from it, every one who receives the protection of society owes a return for the benefit, and the fact of living in society renders it indispensable that each should be bound to observe a certain line of conduct toward the rest. This conduct consists, first, in not injuring the interests of one another; or rather certain interests, which, either by express legal provision or by tacit understanding, ought to be considered as rights; and, secondly, in each person's bearing his share (to be fixed on some equitable principle) of the labours and sacrifices incurred for defending the society or its members from injury and molestation. These conditions society is justified in enforcing, at all costs to those who endeavor to withhold fulfillment. Nor is this all society may do. The acts of an individual may be hurtful to others, or wanting in due consideration for their welfare, without going to the length of violating any of their constituted rights. The offender may then be justly punished by opinion, though not by law. As soon as any part of a person's conduct affects prejudicially the interests of others, society has jurisdiction over it, and the question whether the general welfare will or will not be promoted by interfering with it, becomes open to discussion. But there is no room for entertaining any such question when a person's conduct affects the interests of no persons besides himself, or needs not affect them unless they like (all the persons concerned being of full age, and the ordinary amount of understanding). In all such cases, there should be perfect freedom, legal and social, to do the action and stand the consequences.

(John Stuart Mill, *On Liberty*)

31. The best title for this passage would be

    (A) An Unwritten Contract   (B) Social Obligations
    (C) Public Opinion and the Law   (D) Prerequisites for Liberty
    (E) Principles of Law

32. According to the passage, the conduct of each person in society must be based on which of the following?

   I. Not injuring the rights of others
  II. Promising to propose legislation to bring about social freedom

III. Bearing a share in the defense of society against injury

(A) I only (B) I and II only
(C) II only (D) II and III only
(E) I and III only

33. It can be inferred that the author's concern for individuals and society is that of

(A) An irate citizen (B) A liberal legislator
(C) An uninformed commentator (D) A philosophical historian
(E) An emotional observer

34. The passage is probably intended to

(A) Argue an unpopular point of view
(B) Suggest the weaknesses of society
(C) Present ways of dealing with social misfits
(D) Provide historical information about the evolution of society
(E) Clarify the individual's role in society

35. According to the passage, an individual should be punished by opinion and not by law when

(A) His acts, though hurtful to others, do not violate another's constituted rights
(B) He doesn't bear his fair share in the defense of society
(C) His acts are hurtful to his own legal rights
(D) He refuses to accept the legal and social consequences of his actions
(E) He prevents society from enforcing laws against others

(Reprinted in part with permission of the American Chemical Society)

Color is an important facet of nature, influencing the life of almost every creature. Color is ultimately a sensation in our minds, associated with light striking our eyes. The
5 human eye has special cells (cone cells) containing three different pigments, which respond differently to different colors. Color is perceived according to the relative excitation of these pigments.

10 In nature, animals employ colors for many purposes. The most obvious is camouflage, which allows creatures to blend into their background and avoid detection. Often the animal's color changes with the seasons to
15 coincide with foliage changes. A classic example of the selective advantage of camouflage is found in English peppered moths. Normally light in color, black specimens grew more common as 19th century industrial Eng-
20 land burned more coal, which deposited considerable soot on buildings and trees. Of course, birds could more easily see and catch lighter moths against this background. Now approximately 90 percent of the moths in in-
25 dustrial areas of England are dark. A hopeful sign: lighter moths seem to be coming back as air pollution controls become more effective.

Nonetheless, many animals are brightly and conspicuously colored. One purpose of vivid display is warning. Poisonous and ill-tasting creatures use bright, easily recognized patterns as signatures, reminding would-be predators to look but not taste. Predators avoid them, an advantage to both. And if imitation is the sincerest form of flattery, it can also be a key to survival. So effective are color patterns in protecting bad-tasting and poisonous insects, that completely harmless varieties sometimes mimic these patterns. The bluffers are afforded the same protection as their undesirable relatives, so long as they do not become too numerous. Certain moths and butterflies make more bizarre use of color. Large eye-like markings on their wings apparently frighten, or at least confuse, birds and other predators. Similar markings are found on some fish. Some insects use color to disguise themselves as inanimate objects—imitating things ranging from leaves to bird droppings.

Colors play important roles in many animals' mating behavior. Usually color functions either to warn off rivals or to make an individual more attractive in competition for a mate. This is especially obvious when just one sex is highly colored, as are male robins and peacocks.

Man's use of colors dates back probably 150,000 to 200,000 years when primitive men first used red and yellow clays to paint their bodies. Early men also burned bones and teeth to produce black pigments. Other mineral colors soon came into use, made from ores of iron, copper, and lead. Organic colors were obtained from insects, other animals, and plants. Chalk and lime were used for white. Reds were made from the root of madder plants, the dried bodies of female cochineal insects, and cinnabar. Blue came from copper minerals and the indigo plant. Typically these substances were first washed and dried, then mixed into oils for use in crafts such as painting, pottery, and textiles.

Tyrian purple's story is fascinating. This brilliant purple dye, closely related to indigo, is prepared by oxidizing secretions from certain mollusks (Murex) found in the Eastern Mediterranean. According to one report, 240,000 of the sea creatures were required for one ounce of dye. The dye was, in any case, very expensive, the equivalent of about $7,500 per ounce and traditionally was associated with royalty. Hence the expression,

"born to the purple." Jealous Roman rulers
85 passed a law forbidding anyone outside the
court to wear purple robes, under threat of
death. This dye helped establish the Phoeni-
cian city of Tyre as an ancient trading center.

In many cases, colors took on mystic and
90 religious significance. The Greeks apparently assigned colors to what they believed were
the four basic elements: earth (blue), water
(green), fire (red), and air (yellow). In the
Hindu Upanishads* one reads, "What is true
95 is the three colors. The red color of the sun
is the color of fire, the white of water, the
black of earth. . ." Many American Indian
tribes attached mystical significance to certain colors. Heraldry, which originated in
100 Germany in the 12th Century and later
came to England, evolved its own color symbolism; for example, gold for honor, red for
courage, blue for piety. A modern example of
such symbolism, the colors of capes on
105 academic gowns identify one's academic area
of specialization.
(Paul Seybold, *Color in Nature*)

*Treatises composed between the 8th and 6th Centuries
B.C. and first written in A.D. 1300.

36. Which of the following titles best summarizes the content of the passage?

(A) Color in Nature
(B) Historical Uses of Color
(C) Man's Use of Color
(D) Color: Its Usefulness for All Living Things
(E) Color: In the Mind of the Beholder

37. The author suggests that an animal's color

(A) May be altered by its environment
(B) May be a means of classification
(C) May be the result of pigmentation in the skin that changes with the seasons
(D) May be seen by human eyes, but not by the eyes of animals
(E) May be unique to each species as a signature is unique to each human being

38. It can be inferred from the information in the passage that colorblindness may result when

(A) Light strikes the human eye at an acute angle
(B) The human brain fails to respond to pigments
(C) The cone cells of the human eye lack one of the three necessary pigments
(D) The cone cells of the human eye become excited
(E) Color wave forms are too intense

39. The author suggests that survival of certain creatures who depend upon camouflage is related to

(A) The number of predators in the environment
(B) Their ability to destroy their enemies
(C) Their ability to blend into the environment
(D) Their mating behavior
(E) Their size

40. Which of the following statements regarding color (is) [are not] supported by the passage?

    I.   An ancient trading center, Tyre, flourished because of its proximity to the source of a rare natural dye

   II. Many arts and crafts expanded due to the discoveries of natural pigments and dyes

 III. Colors play a significant role in the customs and beliefs of many cultures

 IV. Mimicry occurs only in animals that wish to display their color as a warning to predators

(A) I only   (B) II only
(C) III only   (D) IV only
(E) I and II only

Skill Builder—Analogies

Each question below contains a related pair of words or phrases followed by five lettered pairs of words or phrases. Select the answer that best expresses a relationship similar to that expressed in the original pair. The answers will be reviewed in televised Verbal Lesson Five or by your classroom teacher.

Example:

PURSUE: CATCH::

(A) occur: happen   (B) eat: drink
(C) track: overtake   (D) apprehend: chase
(E) contest: victory

	A	B	C	D	E
	○	○	●	○	○

---

1. HOSPITALITY: GUEST::

    (A) joy: comedian   (B) housewarming: hostess
    (C) care: patient   (D) courtesy: chivalry
    (E) Christmas: Santa Claus

2. SCORE: MUSIC::

    (A) points: winning   (B) prose: poetry
    (C) choreography: dancing   (D) model: sculpture
    (E) frame: painting

3. NIBBLE: DEVOUR::

    (A) creep: streak   (B) drench: dehydrate
    (C) chill: thaw   (D) charm: repulse
    (E) frown: moan

4. LUBRICANT: FRICTION::

    (A) grease: oil   (B) refrigerant: heat
    (C) thermometer: temperature   (D) decongestant: medication
    (E) propellant: projectile

5. PERMISSION: AUTHORIZATION::

    (A) interminable: periodic   (B) ban: sanction
    (C) applause: approval   (D) morality: taboo
    (E) dubiety: uncertainty

Reading Comprehension

Following each passage is a question or group of questions based on its content. Select the best answer to each question. The answers will be reviewed in televised Verbal Lesson Five or by your classroom teacher.

Exercise A: Physical Science

The surface of most glaciers is dirty, from the numerous pebbles and sand that lie upon it, and which are heaped together the more the ice under them and among them melts
5   away. The ice of the surface has been partially destroyed and rendered crumbly. In the depths of the crevasses ice is seen of a purity and clearness with which nothing that we are acquainted with on the plains can be
10 compared. From its purity it shows a splendid blue, like that of the sky, only with a greenish hue. Crevasses in which pure ice is visible in the interior occur of all sizes; in the beginning they form slight cracks in which a knife can
15 scarcely be inserted; becoming gradually enlarged to chasms, hundreds or even thousands of feet in length, and 20, 50, and as much as a 100 feet in breadth, while some of them are immeasurably deep. Their vertical
20 dark blue walls of crystal ice, glistening with moisture from the trickling water, form one of the most splendid spectacles that nature can present to us; but, at the same time, a spectacle strongly impregnated with the ex-
25 citement of danger, and only enjoyable by the traveller who feels perfectly free from the slightest tendency to giddiness. The tourist must know how, with the aid of well-nailed shoes and a pointed Alpenstock, to stand even
30 on slippery ice, and at the edge of a vertical precipice the foot of which is lost in the darkness of night, and at an unknown depth. Such crevasses cannot always be evaded in crossing the glacier; at the lower part of the Mer de
35 Glace, for instance, where it is usually crossed by travellers, we are compelled to travel along some extent of precipitous banks of ice that are occasionally only four to six feet in breadth, and on each side of which is such a
40 blue abyss. Many a traveller, who has crept along the steep rocky slopes without fear, there feels his heart sink, and cannot turn his eyes from the yawning chasm, for he must first carefully select every step for his feet. And
45 yet these blue chasms, which lie open and exposed in the daylight, are by no means the worst dangers of the glacier; though, indeed, we are so organised that a danger which we perceive, and which therefore we can safely
50 avoid, frightens us far more than one which

we know to exist, but which is veiled from our eyes. So also it is with glacier chasms. In the lower part of the glacier they yawn before us, threatening death and destruction, and
55 lead us, timidly collecting all our presence of mind, to shrink from them; thus accidents seldom occur. On the upper part of the glacier, on the contrary, the surface is covered with snow; this, when it falls thickly, soon arches
60 over the narrower crevasses of a breadth of from four to eight feet, and forms bridges which quite conceal the crevasse, so that the traveller only sees a beautiful plane snow surface before him. If the snow bridges are
65 thick enough, they will support a man; but they are not always so, and these are the places where men, and even chamois are so often lost. These dangers may readily be guarded against if two or three men are roped
70 together at intervals of 10 or 12 feet. If then one of them falls into a crevasse, the two others can hold him, and draw him out again.
(Hermann Von Helmholtz, *Ice and Glaciers*)

6. The best title for this passage would be

   (A)   Ice and Glaciers
   (B)   Crossing Crevasses: Techniques
   (C)   Crevasses: Beautiful Yet Dangerous
   (D)   Colorful Glacial Ice
   (E)   Glacial Crevasses

7. According to the passage, a traveller can enjoy the spectacle of a crevasse only if he is

   I. Conscious of the danger of snow-bridges
   II. Capable of standing on slippery ice
   III. Free from the tendency to dizziness

   (A)   I and II only
   (B)   I and III only
   (C)   II and III only
   (D)   III only
   (E)   I, II, and III

8. Which of the following pairs best describes the author's primary purpose in the passage?

   (A)   To analyze and solve
   (B)   To investigate and predict
   (C)   To characterize and encourage
   (D)   To explore and encourage
   (E)   To describe and explain

9. According to the passage, the author's attitude toward glaciers and crevasses is

   (A)   Condescending amusement
   (B)   Scornful indifference
   (C)   Ambivalent concern
   (D)   Respectful awe
   (E)   Aloof cynicism

10. All of the following are specifically mentioned about crevasses except

   (A)   Threaten death and destruction
   (B)   Sometimes immeasurably deep
   (C)   Display a greenish-blue hue
   (D)   Sometimes covered by a snow-bridge
   (E)   Contain heaps of pebbles and sand

Vocabulary Builder

Follow the instructions for each of the exercises. Answer keys are provided at the end of the vocabulary builder section. Before doing the exercises, familiarize *yourself with the* 15 Latin Roots, 15 Greek Roots, *and the* Essential Words.

15 Latin Roots

1. acer, acr .... *sharp, bitter*
2. amat, amic, amor .... *love, friendly*
3. cern, cret .... *separate, distinguish, sift*
4. culp .... *blame, fault*
5. fid .... *faith*
6. fug(it) .... *flee, fly, run away*
7. lev .... *light*
8. libr .... *book*
9. mon, monit .... *warn, advise*
10. mut .... *change*
11. ped .... *foot*
12. rog .... *ask*
13. sanguin .... *blood*
14. torque, tort .... *twist, turn, torment*
15. und .... *wave*

15 Greek Roots

1. acr .... *highest, extreme*
2. aesthe, esthe .... *feel, perceive*
3. canon... *rule*
4. dem... *people*
5. didac .... *teach*
6. eth, ethn.. *race, cultural group*
7. ger, geront .... *old age, old people*
8. hol .... *whole*
9. icon .... *image*
10. macr.. *large, long*
11. olig... *few*
12. onym .... *name*
13. pha(n) .... *show, appear*
14. thanat... *death*
15. xen .... *stranger, foreigner*

Essential Words—Human Relations

1. Adroit—*(Adj)* expert, deft
2. Amicable—*(Adj)* friendly
3. Appease—*(V)* placate, satisfy
4. Contrite—*(Adj)* penitent
5. Deleterious—*(Adj)* harmful

6. Demur—*(V)* to object
7. Dissident—*(Adj)* disagreeing in opinion, character; dissenting
8. Egregious—*(Adj)* flagrant
9. Expatriate—*(V)* to expel (a person) from his native country
10. Malinger—*(V)* feign sickness to avoid work or duty
11. Monastic—*(Adj)* of, relating to, or characteristic of the nature of a monastery, its inhabitants, or their way of life
12. Peccadillo—*(N)* trifling offense
13. Phlegmatic—*(Adj)* not easily aroused to feeling or action, cool, calm
14. Placate—*(V)* satisfy, appease
15. Truculent—*(Adj)* fierce and cruel

Essential Words—World of Practical Affairs

1. Apocryphal—*(Adj)* of doubtful authorship or authenticity
2. Autocracy—*(N)* state of absolute political power
3. Coalesce—*(V)* unite into one body, mass; combine
4. Coup d'etat—*(N)* a sudden action in politics bringing a change in government
5. De facto—*(Adj)* in fact, in reality
6. Emendation—*(N)* an emending, a correction
7. Equitable—*(Adj)* just, fair
8. Felony—*(N)* serious crime
9. Frieze—*(N)* decorative band
10. Platitude—*(N)* trite remark
11. Prosaic—*(Adj)* commonplace
12. Sedition—*(N)* incitement to rebellion
13. Supercilious—*(Adj)* haughtily disdainful
14. Surreptitious—*(Adj)* stealthy, secret
15. Unctuous—*(Adj)* oily, overly suave

Essential Words—Aesthetic-Philosophical

1. Blithesome—*(Adj)* cheerful, in a joyous manner
2. Bourgeois—*(N)* one of the middle class
3. Bucolic—*(Adj)* rustic, rural
4. Cherub—*(N)* celestial being or angelic child
5. Cuneiform—*(Adj)* wedge-shaped
6. Didactic—*(Adj)* instructive
7. Esoteric—*(Adj)* intended for or understood by a select group
8. Ethereal—*(Adj)* delicate, heavenly, light and airy
9. Hedonist—*(N)* a person who lives only for pleasure
10. Nemesis—*(N)* agent of retribution
11. Pathos—*(N)* quality or power of arousing pity
12. Quintessence—*(N)* essential substance, most perfect example of something
13. Ratiocination—*(N)* process of reasoning
14. Symmetrical—*(Adj)* balanced, even
15. Timbre—*(N)* characteristic quality of sound

Essential Words—Science Related

1. Acme—*(N)* highest point
2. Apiary—*(N)* place where bees are kept
3. Cadaverous—*(Adj)* pale and ghastly
4. Caries—*(N)* decay
5. Crevasse—*(N)* a deep crack in the ice of a glacier
6. Emollient—*(N)* something that softens and soothes
7. Kinetic—*(Adj)* of motion
8. Mercurial—*(Adj)* of mercury, sprightly, fickle
9. Pathological—*(Adj)* dealing with disease, due to or accompanying disease
10. Phylum—*(N)* primary division of plants or animals
11. Precipice—*(N)* a very steep or almost vertical face of a rock or cliff
12. Predator—*(N)* animal or person who lives by preying on other animals or people
13. Predatory—*(Adj)* of or inclined to robbery or plundering
14. Stratified—*(V)* formed in layers
15. Turbid—*(Adj)* muddy, dense, or confused

Exercise 1—Latin Roots

Match the Root in Column A with its meaning in Column B.

Column A		Column B	
1.	acer, acr	(A)	flee, fly, run away
2.	amat, amic, amor	(B)	wave
3.	cern, cret	(C)	blame, fault
4.	culp	(D)	sharp, bitter
5.	fid	(E)	twist, turn, torment
6.	fug(it)	(F)	faith
7.	lev	(G)	blood
8.	libr	(H)	love, friendly
9.	mon, monit	(I)	light
10.	mut	(J)	book
11.	ped	(K)	change
12.	rog	(L)	warn, advise
13.	sanguin	(M)	separate, distinguish, sift
14.	torque, tort	(N)	foot
15.	und	(O)	ask

1. _____   6. _____   11. _____

2. _____   7. _____   12. _____

3. _____   8. _____   13. _____

4. _____   9. _____   14. _____

5. _____   10. _____   15. _____

Exercise 2—Greek Roots

Match the Root in Column A with its meaning in Column B.

Column A		Column B	
1.	acr	(A)	death
2.	aesthe, esthe	(B)	whole

122

3. canon	(C) name
4. dem	(D) old age, old people
5. didac	(E) large, long
6. eth, ethn	(F) few
7. ger, geront	(G) people
8. hol	(H) image
9. icon	(I) race, cultural group
10. macr	(J) show, appear
11. olig	(K) feel, perceive
12. onym	(L) rule
13. pha(n)	(M) stranger, foreigner
14. thanat	(N) highest, extreme
15. xen	(O) teach

1. _____ 6. _____ 11. _____

2. _____ 7. _____ 12. _____

3. _____ 8. _____ 13. _____

4. _____ 9. _____ 14. _____

5. _____ 10. _____ 15. _____

Exercise 3

For each of the key words in Exercise 3 select from the list below one word that is most nearly the same in meaning to the key word and one word that is most nearly opposite to the key word. The first one is done for you.

Synonyms

1. acrimony
2. affable
3. artistic
4. authorized
5. censurable
6. circuitous
7. deception
8. disapprobation
9. distinct
10. encumbrance
11. enlargement
12. exonerate
13. ferocious
14. fictitious
15. flagrant
16. foreboding
17. indigenous
18. insight
19. instructive
20. lightness
21. ordinary
22. pernicious
23. pungent
24. ruddy
25. trustworthiness

Antonyms

amiability
attribute
beneficial
candor
commendation
disagreeable
encouragement
entwined
gentle
gravity
hindsight
legitimate
microcosm
negligence
notable
pale
pandemic
praiseworthy
straightforward
sweet
tasteless
unfaithfulness
uninformative
unsanctioned
virtuous

1. Acerbity
KEY WORD

	acer(b)	ity
prefix(es)	root	suffix(es)

the quality of sharpness, bitterness	sourness of taste; harshness of manner, severity
literal meaning	definition

acrimony	amiability
synonym	antonym

2. Acrid
KEY WORD

	acr	id
prefix(es)	root	suffix(es)

sharp, bitter	sharp, bitter, or stinging to the mouth, eyes, skin, or nose; irritating in manner
literal meaning	definition

synonym	antonym

3. Admonition
KEY WORD

ad	monit	ion
prefix(es)	root	suffix(es)

the act of warning	mild censure; cautionary advice
literal meaning	definition

synonym	antonym

4. Aesthetic
KEY WORD

	aesthe(t)	ic
prefix(es)	root	suffix(es)

having the nature to perceive	pertaining to a sense of the beautiful; showing good taste
literal meaning	definition

synonym	antonym

124

5. Amicable
KEY WORD

prefix(es)	amic	able
	root	suffix(es)

lovely, friendly	having or showing a friendly attitude; peaceable
literal meaning	definition

synonym	antonym

6. Apocryphal
KEY WORD

apo	cryph	al
prefix(es)	root	suffix(es)

hidden away	of questionable authenticity; false, counterfeit
literal meaning	definition

synonym	antonym

7. Canonical
KEY WORD

prefix(es)	canon	ic/al*
	root	suffix(es)

pertaining to rule(s)	relating to canon law; recognized; accepted
literal meaning	definition

synonym	antonym

*Sometimes more than a single suffix is found in a single word
canon: rule + *ic:* pertaining to + *al:* pertaining to

8. Culpable
KEY WORD

prefix(es)	culpa	ble
	root	suffix(es)

fault, blame	deserving blame or censure
literal meaning	definition

synonym	antonym

9. Deleterious
KEY WORD

prefix(es)	deleter	(i)ous
	root	suffix(es)

capable of hurt, injury	harmful to health or well-being; injurious
literal meaning	definition

synonym	antonym

10. Didactic
KEY WORD

prefix(es)	didact	ic
	root	suffix(es)

having to do with teaching	intended to teach; preaching or moralizing
literal meaning	definition

synonym	antonym

11. Discernment
KEY WORD

dis	cern	ment
prefix(es)	root	suffix(es)

the act of sifting apart (to separate by sifting)	keenness of discrimination; acuteness of judgment and understanding
literal meaning	definition

synonym	antonym

12. Discrete
KEY WORD

dis	cret(e)	
prefix(es)	root	suffix(es)

separated	separate; not attached to others; made up of distinct parts
literal meaning	definition

synonym	antonym

13. Egregious*
KEY WORD

e	greg(i)	ous
prefix(es)	root	suffix(es)

out of the herd	outstanding for undesirable qualities; remarkably bad
literal meaning	definition

synonym	antonym

*Egregious once denoted positive qualities such as "distinguished" or "outstanding." Current usage denotes a derogatory sense.

14. Endemic
KEY WORD

en	dem	ic
prefix(es)	root	suffix(es)

prevalent in people	peculiar to a particular people or locality
literal meaning	definition

synonym	antonym

15. Exculpate
KEY WORD

ex	culp	ate
prefix(es)	root	suffix(es)

to remove blame	to free from blame; declare or prove guiltless
literal meaning	definition

synonym	antonym

16. Fidelity
KEY WORD

	fid(el)	ity
prefix(es)	root	suffix(es)

faithfulness	observance of or faithfulness to duties, obligations, or vows; steadfast loyalty
literal meaning	definition

synonym	antonym

17. Impediment
KEY WORD

im	ped(i)*	ment
prefix(es)	root	suffix(es)

an entanglement of the feet

literal meaning

an obstruction, hindrance, or obstacle; some physical defect, especially a defect in speech

definition

synonym

antonym

*ped (foot) is the source of many English words

18. Levity
KEY WORD

	lev	ity
prefix(es)	root	suffix(es)

lacking weight

literal meaning

attitude or behavior lacking seriousness; fickleness

definition

synonym

antonym

19. Macrocosm
KEY WORD

	macro/cosm	
prefix(es)	root	suffix(es)

the large world

literal meaning

the universe itself, or the concept of the universe; any large complex entity

definition

synonym

antonym

20. Pedestrian
KEY WORD

	ped(estri)	an
prefix(es)	root	suffix(es)

one who goes on foot

literal meaning

(N) a person traveling on foot; a walker; (Adj) going or performed on foot; commonplace, undistinguished

definition

synonym

antonym

21. Premonition
KEY WORD

pre	monit	ion
prefix(es)	root	suffix(es)

the act of warning before

a warning in advance; a feeling that something will happen

literal meaning	definition

synonym	antonym

22. Sanguine
KEY WORD

	sanguin(e)	
prefix(es)	root	suffix(es)

blood

of the color of blood; red; eagerly optimistic; cheerful

literal meaning	definition

synonym	antonym

23. Subterfuge
KEY WORD

subter	fug(e)	
prefix(es)	root	suffix(es)

to flee in secret (from Latin: subter– [secretly, underneath] + fugere – [to flee])

any plan, action, or device used to hide one's true objective

literal meaning	definition

synonym	antonym

24. Tortuous
KEY WORD

	tort(u)	ous
prefix(es)	root	suffix(es)

characterized by twisting

not direct; highly involved; complex; full of twists, turns, or bends

literal meaning	definition

synonym	antonym

25. Truculent
_____
KEY WORD

truc(ulent)

| _____ | _____ | _____ |
| prefix(es) | root | suffix(es) |

fierce, savage (from the Latin: trux)	fierce, cruel, savage
literal meaning	definition

| _____ | _____ |
| synonym | antonym |

Exercise 4—Root Words and Meanings

Fill in the blanks with the correct words.

1. The root _____ is found in *anonymous*.

   ANONYMOUS means _____ .

2. The root _____ is found in *demagog*.

   DEMAGOG *means* _____.

3. The root _____ is found in *diffident*.

   DIFFIDENT means _____ .

4. The root _____ is found in *euthanasia*.

   EUTHANASIA means _____ .

5. The root _____ is found in *holocaust*.

   HOLOCAUST means _____ .

6. The root _____ is found in *immutable*.

   IMMUTABLE means _____ .

7. The root _____ is found in *premonition*.

   PREMONITION means _____ .

8. The root _____ is found in *quadruped*.

   QUADRUPED means _____ .

9. The root _____ is found in *undulate*.

   UNDULATE means _____ .

10. The root _____ is found in *xenogamy*.

    XENOGAMY means _____ .

Exercise 5—Essential Words

Match each word in Column A with its definition in Column B.

Column A		Column B
1. cadaverous	(A)	agent of retribution
2. caries	(B)	incitement to rebellion

130

3.	egregious	(C)	a correction	
4.	emendation	(D)	trifling offense	
5.	hedonist	(E)	decay	
6.	kinetic	(F)	person who lives only for pleasure	
7.	nemesis	(G)	trite remark	
8.	peccadillo	(H)	of motion	
9.	platitude	(I)	flagrant	
10.	sedition	(J)	pale and ghastly	

1. _____   6. _____

2. _____   7. _____

3. _____   8. _____

4. _____   9. _____

5. _____   10. _____

Exercise 6—Antonyms

Match each word in Column A with the word most nearly opposite in Column B.

Column A

1.	amicable
2.	bourgeois
3.	bucolic
4.	cherub
5.	deleterious
6.	demur
7.	equitable
8.	placate
9.	symmetrical
10.	turbid

Column B

(A)	aristocrat
(B)	uneven
(C)	agree
(D)	urban
(E)	hostile
(F)	agitate
(G)	imp
(H)	beneficial
(I)	clear
(J)	unfair

1. _____   6. _____

2. _____   7. _____

3. _____   8. _____

4. _____   9. _____

5. _____   10. _____

Exercise 7—Sentence Completion

Complete the sentences in Column B by filling in the blank with the correct word from Column A.

Column A   Column B

1. amicable   1. The two students settled their argument in an _____ way.

2. coalesced   2. Cold cream is an _____ for the skin.

3. emollient   3. He was hospitalized for a _____ condition of the blood cells.

4. ethereal

4. The novice took the _____ vows of chastity, poverty, and obedience.

5. monastic

5. She is _____; she never seems to get excited about anything.

6. pathological

6. _____ pirates infested the seas.

7. phlegmatic

7. The thirteen colonies _____ to form a nation.

8. predatory

8. Her dress was the _____ of good taste and style.

9. quintessence

9. The photograph reproduced the _____ beauty of the butterfly.

10. unctuous

10. The group objected to the hypocrite's _____ manner.

Vocabulary Check Test

(Answers will be reviewed in televised Verbal Lesson Five or by your classroom teacher.)

Part A

Choose the word or phrase most nearly opposite to the word in capital letters.

1. QUINTESSENCE: (A) almost obsolete   (B) very thin   (C) most unfortunate   (D) seriously impeded   (E) not essential

2. CULPABLE: (A) digressive   (B) believable   (C) praiseworthy   (D) communicable   (E) touchable

3. PANDEMIC: (A) limited   (B) scenic   (C) influential   (D) exhausting   (E) selfish

4. IMMUTABLE: (A) mortal   (B) practicable   (C) uncomfortable   (D) variable   (E) logical

5. ETHEREAL: (A) tactful   (B) coarse   (C) sensitive   (D) fashionable   (E) obscured

6. COMATOSE: (A) angelic   (B) dangerous   (C) doubtful   (D) animated   (E) unemployed

7. CONTRITE: (A) opposed   (B) brief   (C) impenitent   (D) persuasive   (E) peaceful

8. PATHOLOGICAL: (A) explorative   (B) impatient   (C) controversial   (D) persistent   (E) salutary

9. DEMAGOG: (A) ecclesiastic   (B) peacemaker   (C) horse trader   (D) charlatan   (E) protester

10. PLACATE: (A) enrage   (B) forfeit   (C) excuse   (D) shield   (E) discredit

11. FANTASTIC: (A) malicious   (B) popular   (C) mechanical   (D) radical   (E) realistic

12. PROGNOSTICATION: (A) experience   (B) predilection   (C) mediation
   (D) hindsight   (E) precept

13. ETHICAL: (A) habitual   (B) intricate   (C) immoral
   (D) tolerable   (E) isolated

14. BOURGEOIS: (A) nobility   (B) authority   (C) conservative
   (D) nincompoop   (E) infantry

15. ESOTERIC: (A) flighty   (B) obvious   (C) sluggish
   (D) profuse   (E) lasting

Part B

From the list below choose the word that best completes the analogy by expressing a relationship similar to that expressed in the original pair.

(A) anodyne
(B) apiary
(C) coalescence
(D) coup d'etat
(E) emendation

(F) felony
(G) immutableness
(H) premonition
(I) serration
(J) undulation

16. Wolf: lair:: bee: _____

17. Troupe: acting:: junta: _____

18. Motion: amendment:: literary work: _____

19. Berlin Wall: segregation:: Common Market: _____

20. Fork: prong:: saw: _____

21. Speed: velocity:: wave: _____

22. Sorrow: consolation:: pain: _____

23. Mystery: solution:: hindsight: _____

24. Insinuation: camouflage:: change: _____

25. Peccadillo: atrocity:: misdemeanor: _____

Part C

From the list below select the words that best fit the meaning or context of the sentence.

(1) admonish
(2) amicable
(3) canonical
(4) congenital
(5) endemic

(6) ethical
(7) ethnological
(8) euthanasia
(9) pecuniary
(10) seditious

26. The _____ writings of the medical profession forbid doctors from practicing _____

by painlessly inducing death, however merciful the reasons.

133

27. Large, _____ debts forced him to abandon his _____ study of the origins of tribal rituals.

28. Judges often _____ prospective jurors about revealing any personal _____ beliefs that would interfere with their impartiality.

29. The cruelty of the captain caused a wave of _____ whisperings to sweep through the once _____ crew.

30. Some inheritable diseases are _____, prevalent in or peculiar to a particular locality or people; some hereditary; some _____, existing at birth.

Simulated Test of Standard Written English

TEST I
Time—30 Minutes

This exercise is designed to test your ability to recognize standard written English. Standard written English is the form that is accepted more often in writing than in speaking. It is used in academic and technical writing and in certain literature.

Part I (Questions 1-25)

Directions:

Some of the following sentences contain errors in grammar, usage, diction (choice of words), or idiom (a phrase or expression characteristic to the language).

Some of the sentences are correct.
Errors, if present, will be found in the underlined, lettered sections (A, B, C, and D).

No sentence contains more than one error. If you locate an error, indicate on your answer sheet the underlined section that contains the error, and that must be changed in order to correct the sentence. If there is no error in the sentence, choose E.

Example:

I. I can't do <u>nothing</u> <u>about</u> the problem
           A   B

   <u>unless</u> you <u>are</u> willing to help me. <u>No error.</u>
    C   D   E

Sample Answers:

I.   A   B   C   D   E
    ●   ○   ○   ○   ○

---

1. The manager <u>tried to hire</u> <u>only</u> those workers <u>which were</u> skilled, but often he <u>had</u> to fill the
              A   B   C   D
   vacancies with untrained people. <u>No error.</u>
                                E

2. Barbara and George sat under the old elm, <u>talking quietly</u> <u>while</u> the others <u>played</u> a spirited game
                                             A   B   C
   of tennis <u>near the river</u>. <u>No error.</u>
             D   E

3. The <u>clouds covered</u> the moon <u>so thickly</u> that we <u>couldn't hardly</u> find our <u>way back</u> to the cottage.
             A   B   C   D
   <u>No error.</u>
     E

4. <u>During the Cuban Revolution</u>, many professionals <u>came</u> to the United States and <u>must find</u> un-
             A   B   C
   skilled positions in order <u>to support</u> their families. <u>No error.</u>
                          D   E

5. She is greatly admired by her superiors because of her honesty, enthusiasm, and she dedicates
      A   B   C   D
   herself to her work. No error.
                         E

6. Most of the evenings were occupied with playing chess and they would listen to records. No error.
        A   B   C   D   E

7. The reporters were taught to be concise and only to report the facts of each incident. No error.
                   A   B   C   D   E

8. Neither the students nor the teacher agree with the principal's decision to cancel the program.
   A   B   C   D
   No error.
   E

9. The right of workers to bargain collectively with their employer is protected under the National
         A   B   C   D
   Labor Relations Act. No error.
                         E

10. I read in yesterday's newspaper where the mayor has been reelected for the third time. No error.
              A   B   C   D   E

11. While suffering from appendicitis, the nursing staff of the local hospital was warm and friendly.
                     A   B   C   D
    No error.
    E

12. After the match, she was so thirsty that she would have drank the contents of the cooler if her
                          A   B
    coach had not restrained her. No error.
          C   D   E

13. I was a better student than him, but I was no match for him when we competed in athletic events.
                             A   B   C   D
    No error.
    E

14. He never had been frightened of snakes until he was bitten by a copperhead last fall. No error.
            A   B   C   D   E

15. Both are informative articles, but this one is best. No error.
    A   B   C   D   E

16. The affect of the newscast was stunning; some listeners were angry and others were shocked.
          A   B   C   D
    No error.
    E

17. In spite of higher fuel costs, my car has been drove more miles this year than last. No error.
    A   B   C   D   E

18. The university is proud of their productive, intelligent students, many of whom earn national
                        A   B   C   D
    recognition. No error.
                  E

136

19. I find <u>making</u> that <u>kind of a</u> decision difficult, <u>especially</u> with <u>so little</u> information available to me.
        A   B   C   D
    <u>No error.</u>
    E

20. <u>Dining</u> in restaurants, although much <u>more expensive</u> than dining <u>at home</u>, often <u>provide</u> oppor-
    A   B   C   D
    <u>tunities</u> to try new foods. <u>No error.</u>
                                  E

21. The <u>requirement</u> <u>of the handicapped</u> should <u>be considered</u> <u>when designing</u> libraries, schools, and
            A   B   C   D
    other public structures. <u>No error.</u>
                             E

22. <u>Any member</u> <u>of the cheerleading squad</u> <u>whose</u> academic record <u>are</u> low must be dropped from
        A   B   C   D
    the squad. <u>No error.</u>
              E

23. Thomas Alva Edison, <u>a prolific scientist,</u> <u>discovered</u> the <u>electric light bulb</u> <u>and</u> the phonograph.
                          A   B   C   D
    <u>No error.</u>
    E

24. Jimmy <u>must of</u> <u>lied</u> <u>about his age</u> to get <u>into the Air Force.</u> <u>No error.</u>
            A   B   C   D   E

25. <u>It's sometimes</u> <u>easier</u> <u>to do the work</u> oneself than <u>supervising</u> someone else. <u>No error.</u>
    A   B   C   D   E

Part II (Questions 26-40)

The sentences in this section test correctness and effectiveness of expression.

Directions:

In each of the following sentences, some part of the sentence is underlined. After the sentence you will find five ways of phrasing the underlined part. Choose the answer that creates the most effective sentence, one that is clear and concise, without awkwardness, and indicate your choice on your answer sheet. In selecting answers, follow the rules of standard written English, but do *not* select an answer that alters the meaning of the original sentence.

Answer A is always the same as the underlined section. Choose A if you think the original sentence requires no change.

Example:	Sample
Mrs. Polay <u>preparing</u> the patient for his operation.	A B C D E ○ ○ ○ ○ ●
(A) preparing (C) have prepared (E) prepares	(B) are preparing (D) with preparation

26. Michael introduced himself to a nurse <u>who worked at the hospital where he was born, when he was nineteen years old.</u>

    (A) who worked at the hospital where he was born, when he was nineteen years old.
    (B) who had worked at the hospital where he was born nineteen years ago.
    (C) working at the hospital nineteen years ago where he was born.
    (D) who worked when he was nineteen years old at the hospital where he was born.
    (E) working where he was born, when he was nineteen.

27. The circus clown tipped his hat to the little girl and <u>waving happily to the other children in the group.</u>

    (A) waving happily to the other children in the group.
    (B) waved to the children happily.
    (C) waved to the children happily in the group.
    (D) was waving happily to the other children in the group.
    (E) waved happily to the other children in the group.

28. <u>The six-day work week not only has been reduced</u> to one of five days but also, in some instances, to one of four days.

    (A) The six-day work week not only has been reduced
    (B) Not only the six-day work week has been reduced
    (C) Not only has the six-day work week been reduced
    (D) The six-day work week has not only been reduced
    (E) The six-day work week has been reduced not only

29. <u>When one attends a movie these days, you often find</u> that it is expensive and artistically inferior.

    (A) When one attends a movie these days, you often find
    (B) When you go to a movie these days, one sometimes finds
    (C) If you went to a movie these days, you found
    (D) If you go to a movie now, one can find
    (E) When you go to a movie these days, you often find

30. The critics were bored with the play <u>while I found it absorbing.</u>

    (A) while I found it absorbing.
    (B) and I found it absorbing.
    (C) but I found it absorbing.
    (D) but as it happened, I found it absorbing.
    (E) nonetheless, I saw it anyway.

31. A complete investigation into the causes of the accident should lead to improved standards and <u>new operating procedures will result.</u>

    (A) new operating procedures will result.
    (B) different operating procedures will result.
    (C) should result in new operating procedures.
    (D) such an understanding will result in new procedures.
    (E) operating procedures that are new resulted.

32. Diving before the judges for the first time, <u>terror slowly overcame the contestant and he could not move his body.</u>

    (A) terror slowly overcame the contestant and he could not move his body.
    (B) the body could not be moved by the contestant because he was slowly overcome by terror.
    (C) the contestant was slowly overcome by terror and he could not move his body.
    (D) the contestant's terrorized body could not be moved.
    (E) the contestant's body could not be moved since it was terrorized.

33. Many adults are giving up smoking, but <u>some delaying it.</u>

    (A) some delaying it.
    (B) some are delaying it.
    (C) it is delayed by some of them.
    (D) it is being delayed.
    (E) some having delayed it.

34. Large areas of the United States are being developed in ways that ignore extremes in weather, tax underground water sources, <u>and nature's ecological balance is weakened.</u>

    (A) and nature's ecological balance is weakened.
    (B) and weaken nature's ecological balance.
    (C) while weakening nature's ecological balance.
    (D) but still continue the weakening of nature's ecological balance.
    (E) and because of this nature's ecological balance is weakened.

35. The early pioneers embarked on their extraordinary <u>journey, but they were</u> properly outfitted.

    (A) journey, but they were
    (B) journey, where they were
    (C) journey only when they were
    (D) journey only when being
    (E) journey because it was

36. <u>It almost seems impossible</u> to finish writing the manuscript by December.

    (A) It almost seems impossible
    (B) It is almost seemingly impossible
    (C) Seemingly impossible it is
    (D) It seems impossible, almost,
    (E) It seems almost impossible

37. <u>I originally had planned to finish the bicycle trip with my brother and she</u> before embarking on a mountain climbing expedition.

    (A) I originally had planned to finish the bicycle trip with my brother and she
    (B) Originally I had planned to finish the bicycle trip with my brother and she
    (C) I originally had planned to finish the bicycle trip with my brother and her
    (D) I had planned originally to finish the bicycle trip with my brother and she
    (E) I had planned to finish the bicycle trip originally with my brother and her

38. <u>The reason I selected this project is</u> because it posed a unique challenge.

    (A) The reason I selected this project is
    (B) I selected this project
    (C) The reason that I selected this project is
    (D) One of the reasons why I selected this project is
    (E) My reason for selecting this project is

39. Tom requested that the videotapes be sent immediately and <u>the booklets should be prepared for mailing the next day.</u>

    (A) the booklets should be prepared for mailing the next day.
    (B) the booklets ought to be prepared for mailing the next day.
    (C) the booklets most likely should be prepared for mailing the next day.
    (D) the booklets be prepared for mailing the next day.
    (E) the booklets are prepared for mailing the next day.

40. William runs faster <u>than any boy in his class.</u>

    (A)   than any boy in his class.
    (B)   than anyone in his class.
    (C)   than any other boy in his class.
    (D)   than those boys in his class.
    (E)   than all boys in his class.

Part III (Questions 41-50)

The remaining questions are similar to those in Part I.

41. <u>None</u> of his relatives <u>really</u> understood the full <u>extent</u> <u>of his difficulty</u> or <u>how desperate he really</u>
    A   B   C   D
<u>was.</u> <u>No error.</u>
       E

42. <u>She</u> is the one <u>to whom</u> <u>you</u> <u>should mail</u> the package. <u>No error.</u>
    A   B   C   D   E

43. The president complained that neither the secretary <u>nor</u> the treasurer <u>have given</u> a report <u>to the</u>
                                             A   B   C
<u>membership</u> <u>this year.</u> <u>No error.</u>
         D   E

44. Robert Redford and Jane Fonda, known for their <u>credible</u> performances, <u>are considered</u> two of
                                                     A   B
the most <u>notorious</u> film stars <u>in the country.</u> <u>No error.</u>
         C   D   E

45. <u>In order to settle the matter,</u> I <u>will accept</u> <u>either</u> six new chairs or <u>having the old ones reupholstered.</u>
            A   B   C   D
<u>No error.</u>
  E

46. The nation is <u>in the midst of</u> a recession <u>with unemployment rates</u> <u>climbing</u> <u>at an alarming rate.</u>
                    A   B   C   D
<u>No error.</u>
  E

47. Ray is one <u>of those boys</u> <u>who</u> <u>always</u> <u>excel</u> in school. <u>No error.</u>
            A   B   C   D   E

48. A number <u>of students</u> <u>has</u> <u>already</u> registered for the course <u>that</u> will start in September. <u>No error.</u>
            A   B   C   D   E

49. No one but <u>you and I</u> <u>knows</u> <u>who</u> the <u>culprit is.</u> <u>No error.</u>
          A   B   C   D   E

50. Dr. Jones told <u>both</u> <u>them and us</u> about the dangers of <u>our</u> smoking <u>too</u> many cigarettes. <u>No error.</u>
              A   B   C   D   E

Simulated Test of Standard Written English

TEST II

Time—30 Minutes

This exercise is designed to test your ability to recognize standard written English. Standard written English is the form that is accepted more often in writing than in speaking. It is used in academic and technical writing and in certain literature.

Part I (Questions 1-25)

Directions:

Some of the following sentences contain errors in grammar, usage, diction (choice of words), or idiom (a phrase or expression characteristic to the language).

Some of the sentences are correct.
Errors, if present, will be found in the underlined, lettered sections (A, B, C, and D).

No sentence contains more than one error. If you locate an error, indicate on your answer sheet the underlined section that contains the error, and that must be changed in order to correct the sentence. If there is no error in the sentence, choose E.

Example:		Sample Answers:

I.   I can't do nothing about the problem
              A   B
   unless you are willing to help me. No error.
        C   D   E

I.   A   B   C   D   E
     ●   ○   ○   ○   ○

---

1. In the depression and drought years of the 1930s, more than a third of the American population
       A   B
   receiving assistance payments and thousands lost their farms. No error.
   C   D   E

2. Practically everyone who was invited to the reception was able to except the invitation. No error.
   A   B   C   D   E

3. Alice is one of those many girls who always wins honors in school. No error.
                     A   B   C   D   E

4. While walking down the platform, the subway came suddenly to an abrupt stop and some pas-
   A   B   C   D
   sengers were injured. No error.
                        E

5. The naturalization of one married person does not automatically result in the naturalization of
                        A   B   C
   their spouse. No error.
   D   E

141

6. One of the principal reasons behind his success was that he seemed real enthusiastic about his
            A   B   C   D
   work. No error.
         E

7. Neither Fred nor his friends has received the necessary medical inoculations required for the
                A   B   C   D
   journey. No error.
           E

8. Although William considers himself a magician, he has never made a career of it. No error.
   A   B   C   D   E

9. Be sure to have the girls call me when they are already to leave for school. No error.
   A   B   C   D   E

10. Because of the extreme weather conditions, there will be less oranges from Florida this season.
       A   B   C   D
    No error.
      E

11. Tony only studied what was important; he didn't waste his time. No error.
         A   B   C   D   E

12. I asked my friend to give the opera ticket to whomever wants it. No error.
                     A   B   C   D   E

13. They are not likely to award him damages for his foot which was injured while climbing Pikes Peak.
                 A   B   C   D
    No error.
      E

14. No one but you and I knows that the mayor will formally announce his resignation in two weeks.
           A   B C   D
    No error.
      E

15. Everyone finished his chores early except William and me, so when it came time for us children
                     A   B   C
    to share the cookies, it was already eaten. No error.
                          D   E

16. Almost immediately I regretted that I acted so hastily in selecting the clothes for my new wardrobe.
    A   B   C   D
    No error.
      E

17. Every one of the politicans have viewed his disclosure as a cynical ploy. No error.
                              A   B   C   D   E

18. For hundreds of years, mothers and fathers have used nursery rhymes to quiet a baby when he
                                  A   B
    is restless, to make him laugh, and to encourage him to talk. No error.
                C   D   E

19. When the time comes to choose an occupation, it should be important to match interests with
    A   B   C   D

142

abilities. <u>No error.</u>
            E

20. I <u>will use</u> the reward <u>either</u> to take <u>a vacation</u> or <u>for completing</u> my flying lessons. <u>No error.</u>
        A   B   C   D   E

21. <u>Neither</u> of my friends <u>has had</u> the mumps; <u>however,</u> I have had <u>them.</u> <u>No error.</u>
        A   B   C   D   E

22. No one <u>has discovered</u> the <u>reason</u> for <u>him</u> <u>withdrawing</u> from the race. <u>No error.</u>
            A   B   C   D   E

23. Eugenia <u>did not object</u> <u>to giving</u> a piece of cake to <u>whomever</u> wanted <u>one.</u> <u>No error.</u>
                A   B   C   D   E

24. Having <u>run</u> up the stairs of the <u>capitol,</u> Tom quickly apprehended the thief, a deed for <u>which</u> he
            A   B   C
received a plaque and fifty dollars <u>besides.</u> <u>No error.</u>
                                        D   E

25. Because I <u>should of been</u> home <u>at midnight,</u> Father <u>objected</u> to <u>my</u> driving his car on weekends.
                    A   B   C   D
<u>No error.</u>
    E

Part II (Questions 26-40)

The sentences in this section test correctness and effectiveness of expression.

Directions:

In each of the following sentences, some part of the sentence is underlined. After the sentence you will find five ways of phrasing the underlined part. Choose the answer that creates the most effective sentence, one that is clear and concise, without awkwardness, and indicate your choice on your answer sheet. In selecting answers, follow the rules of standard written English, but do *not* select an answer that alters the meaning of the original sentence.

Answer A is always the same as the underlined section. Choose A if you think the original sentence requires no change.

Example:	Sample
Mrs. Polay <u>preparing</u> the patient for his operation.	A B C D E ○ ○ ○ ○ ●
(A) preparing	(B) are preparing
(C) have prepared	(D) with preparation
(E) prepares	

26. The sport of skiing <u>owes much development and popularity to the Norwegians.</u>

    (A) owes much development and popularity to the Norwegians.
    (B) depends a lot on the Norwegians for its development and popularity.
    (C) developed due to the Norwegians and is popular.
    (D) owes much of its development and popularity to the Norwegians.
    (E) is popular and developed since the Norwegians.

143

27. Thrilled at the thought of going to the dance, <u>her troubles were quickly forgotten and she made an appointment at the beauty salon.</u>

    (A)   her troubles were quickly forgotten and she made an appointment at the beauty salon.
    (B)   she made an appointment at the beauty salon because her troubles were forgotten.
    (C)   she quickly forgot her troubles and made an appointment at the beauty salon.
    (D)   quickly she forgot her troubles, and as a result made an appointment at the beauty salon.
    (E)   she quickly forgot her troubles to make an appointment at the beauty salon.

28. Kevin asked, <u>"Will you go to the movies with me"?</u>

    (A)   "Will you go to the movies with me"?
    (B)   "Will you go to the movies with me?"
    (C)   "Will you go to the movies with me?"
    (D)   will you go to the movies with me?
    (E)   "will you go to the movies with me"?

29. If one is feeling adventurous, <u>you can bicycle across the country or canoe down a river.</u>

    (A)   you can bicycle across the country or canoe down a river.
    (B)   you should try bicycling across the country or canoeing down a river.
    (C)   they should try bicycling across the country or canoeing down a river.
    (D)   he can bicycle across the country or try canoeing down a river.
    (E)   he can bicycle across the country or canoe down a river.

30. He told me <u>he attended every meeting concerning the effects of pollution upon that particular species.</u>

    (A)   he attended every meeting concerning the effects of pollution upon that particular species.
    (B)   he had attended every meeting concerning the effects of pollution upon that particular species.
    (C)   he had attended every meeting concerning the affects of pollution upon that particular species.
    (D)   he attended every meeting concerning the effects of pollution upon that particular specie.
    (E)   he had attended every meeting because of the effects of pollution upon that particular species.

31. *The Bridge of San Luis Rey,* <u>which we studied in high school,</u> investigates the lives of diverse characters who are gathered on a suspension bridge in Peru.

    (A)   *The Bridge of San Luis Rey,* which we studied in high school,
    (B)   The Bridge of San Luis Rey which we studied in High School
    (C)   *The Bridge of San Luis Rey* which we studied in high school
    (D)   *The Bridge of San Luis Rey,* that was studied in high school,
    (E)   *The Bridge of San Luis Rey,* about which we studied in high school,

32. <u>The fare for my airline ticket costs more than the hotel.</u>

    (A)   The fare for my airline ticket costs more than the hotel.
    (B)   The fare for my airline ticket cost more than the hotel did.
    (C)   The fare for my airline ticket costs more than any hotel.
    (D)   The fare for my airline ticket costs more than the price of the hotel.
    (E)   The fare which I paid for my airline ticket is more than the hotel.

33. Wasn't it Abraham Lincoln who said, <u>the nation's destiny rests with the people not with the politicians.</u>

    (A)   the nation's destiny rests with the people not with the politicians.
    (B)   The Nation's destiny rests with the people, not with the politicians?
    (C)   "The nation's destiny rests with the people, not with the politicians?"
    (D)   "The nation's destiny rests with the people, not with the politicians."?
    (E)   "The nation's destiny rests with the people, not with the politicians"?

34. Redundancy <u>is when you repeat an idea expressed elsewhere in a sentence.</u>

    (A) is when you repeat an idea expressed elsewhere in a sentence.
    (B) is when you repeat an idea which you expressed elsewhere in a sentence.
    (C) is the repetition of an idea expressed elsewhere in a sentence.
    (D) is where an idea is repeated which was expressed elsewhere in a sentence.
    (E) is an idea which repeats itself as an expression elsewhere in a sentence.

35. <u>Although some fish migrate over a great distance</u> during their journeys make special use of their sense of smell.

    (A) Although some fish migrate over a great distance
    (B) Even though some fish migrate over a great distance and
    (C) Some fish having migrated over great distances and
    (D) Some fish had migrated over great distances
    (E) Some fish migrate over great distances and

36. We rarely perceive more than a minute fraction of the sights and sounds that fall upon our sense <u>organs, the great majority</u> pass us by.

    (A) organs, the great majority
    (B) organs, consequently the great majority
    (C) organs, and as a consequence, the great majority
    (D) organs; while the great majority
    (E) organs; the great majority

37. <u>Published in 1962, Rachel Carson wrote the book *Silent Spring* which had been directed</u> against those people who poison our environment with chemical pesticides.

    (A) Published in 1962, Rachel Carson wrote the book *Silent Spring* which had been directed
    (B) Published in 1962, Rachel Carson wrote the book *Silent Spring* which was directed
    (C) Published in 1962, the book *Silent Spring* by Rachel Carson was directed
    (D) Published in 1962, Rachel Carson had written a book, *Silent Spring,* which was directed
    (E) Published in 1962, the book *Silent Spring* by Rachel Carson was being directed

38. <u>They talked about taking a cruise on their anniversary frequently</u>, but they never did.

    (A) They talked about taking a cruise on their anniversary frequently
    (B) They talked frequently about taking a cruise on their anniversary
    (C) They talked about taking a cruise frequently on their anniversary
    (D) Frequently on their anniversary they talked about taking a cruise
    (E) They had talked about taking a cruise on their anniversary frequently

39. <u>The nervous system is more easily understood</u> if its parts are thought of as separate units that are classified according to the work they do.

    (A) The nervous system is more easily understood
    (B) The nervous system is easier understood
    (C) Nervous systems are more easily understood
    (D) The nervous system is not so difficult
    (E) The nervous system is more easy to understand

40. Most of the members of <u>my family enjoy visiting the zoo and watching the animals, including my grandma.</u>

    (A) my family enjoy visiting the zoo and watching the animals, including my grandma.
    (B) my family, including grandma, enjoys visiting the zoo and watching the animals.
    (C) my family, including my grandma, enjoy visiting the zoo and watching the animals.
    (D) my family enjoys visiting the zoo and watching the animals, including grandma.
    (E) my family, including grandma, enjoy visiting the zoo and to watch the animals.

Part III (Questions 41-50)

The remaining questions are similar to those in Part I.

41. Too many commas in a passage <u>often</u> <u>causes</u> confusion <u>in the reader's</u> mind. <u>No error.</u>
    A   B C   D   E

42. <u>Although</u> he <u>appeared</u> to be a <u>disinterested</u> spectator, I did not believe his <u>incredulous</u> story.
      A   B   C   D
    <u>No error.</u>
     E

43. I <u>cannot</u> help <u>taking</u> Jim's advice even though he paid <u>twice as much</u> for his stereo <u>than</u> I did.
     A   B   C   D
    <u>No error.</u>
     E

44. Mr. Koerner <u>agreed</u> to let <u>Tom and me</u> work in the <u>stationery</u> store for a few hours <u>each week</u>. <u>No</u>
         A   B   C   D E
    <u>error.</u>

45. There <u>are</u> <u>strong feelings</u> of trust and respect <u>between</u> Lisa, Jane, and <u>me</u>. <u>No error.</u>
       A B   C   D E

46. Joann is the <u>only</u> one <u>of our students</u> <u>who</u> <u>has received</u> national recognition for her musical
         A   B   C D
    ability. <u>No error.</u>
       E

47. <u>When swimming</u>, a <u>person</u> is <u>more</u> buoyant in salt water <u>than</u> in fresh water. <u>No error.</u>
       A   B   C   D   E

48. Most <u>people</u> find that earning money is a <u>more</u> difficult task <u>than</u> <u>to spend</u> it. <u>No error.</u>
      A   B   C   D   E

49. The dispute <u>between</u> Alice, William, and <u>me</u> <u>must be resolved</u> if we are <u>to work</u> together effec-
         A   B   C   D
    tively. <u>No error.</u>
      E

50. The typical citizen rarely <u>involves</u> <u>himself</u> personally in a public protest <u>unless</u> <u>they are made</u> to
             A   B   C   D
    feel directly threatened. <u>No error.</u>
           E

Comprehensive Simulated Verbal Examination

Section I
Time—30 Minutes

Segment 1: Opposites
Select the word that is most nearly opposite in meaning to the word or phrase in capital letters. Consider any fine shades of meaning that may exist.

Example:

HOT:

(A) green	(B) river	(C) cold
(D) above	(E) sweet	

A	B	C	D	E
○	○	●	○	○

---

1. INFAMOUS:
   - (A) reputable
   - (B) ingenious
   - (C) noted
   - (D) obscure
   - (E) hungry

2. INTERDICT:
   - (A) eradicate
   - (B) surpass
   - (C) inspect
   - (D) allow
   - (E) amend

3. MITIGATE:
   - (A) interfere
   - (B) endorse
   - (C) aggravate
   - (D) surrender
   - (E) repay

4. INVETERATE:
   - (A) skillfully planned
   - (B) highly valued
   - (C) recently established
   - (D) poorly prepared
   - (E) cleverly evaded

5. DETRIMENT:
   - (A) similarity
   - (B) criticism
   - (C) prudence
   - (D) disruption
   - (E) benefit

6. INSIPID:
   - (A) sparkling
   - (B) unfamiliar
   - (C) confident
   - (D) fiendish
   - (E) occupied

7. TEMERITY:
   - (A) profundity
   - (B) wariness
   - (C) diligence
   - (D) flexibility
   - (E) pessimism

8. INORDINATE:
   - (A) numerical
   - (B) methodical
   - (C) religious
   - (D) luminous
   - (E) restrained

9. ABROGATE:
   - (A) misbehave
   - (B) snub
   - (C) affirm
   - (D) insult
   - (E) disable

10. INVESTITURE:
   - (A) resentment
   - (B) endowment
   - (C) hullabaloo
   - (D) mediation
   - (E) dismissal

11. POTABLE:
   - (A) stimulating
   - (B) undrinkable
   - (C) unwieldy
   - (D) indistinct
   - (E) irascible

12. RISIBLE: (A) solemn   (B) persuasive   (C) noxious
                 (D) haughty   (E) intricate

13. IMPRECATE: (A) misconstrue   (B) initiate   (C) inhibit
                 (D) bless   (E) delete

14. TRUCULENT: (A) suspicious   (B) methodical   (C) imaginative
                 (D) suitable   (E) amiable

15. CASTIGATE: (A) redress   (B) extol   (C) invalidate
                 (D) soothe   (E) pulverize

Segment 2: Sentence Completion

The blanks in each sentence indicate omitted words. Select the word or words that best *fit the meaning of the entire sentence and should be inserted in the blank.*

Example:

On a small farm in an arid climate one should not grow crops that need considerable _____

or _____ to ripen.

(A) fertilizer — attention   (B) space — water
(C) sun — air   (D) tilling — harvesting
(E) weeding — insecticides

A	B	C	D	E
○	●	○	○	○

---

16. Convinced that war was likely, she strove to infuse her own sense of _____ into her colleagues.

    (A) restraint   (B) prudence
    (C) urgency   (D) skepticism
    (E) misjudgment

17. The fairness doctrine requires radio and television stations to broadcast _____ sides of

    important _____ issues.

    (A) ethical — sensitive   (B) opposing — controversial
    (C) obscure — popular   (D) irrelevant — crucial
    (E) cynical — hypothetical

18. The swing of his nature took him from extreme _____ to intense _____.

    (A) languor — energy   (B) temperature — cold
    (C) sullenness — reticence   (D) prudence — caution
    (E) amiability — pleasantness

19. Contrary to popular belief that classical music is too complex, it achieves a _____ that only

    genius can create.

    (A) harmony   (B) simplicity
    (C) intricacy   (D) perspective
    (E) acceptance

20. Man's nature is a bundle of _____; he is individual yet social, unified yet diversified, complete yet incomplete.

   (A) traditions
   (B) anecdotes
   (C) paradoxes
   (D) coincidences
   (E) ideas

21. In the symmetry and grace of the universe man sees not only _____ but also _____.

   (A) confusion — intelligence
   (B) orderliness — beauty
   (C) optimism — pessimism
   (D) unity — antagonism
   (E) conformity — individualism

22. A country artist may show freshness and _____ in his works while his _____ cousin demonstrates sophistication and compactness.

   (A) monotony — old-fashioned
   (B) harmony — rural
   (C) complexity — unsociable
   (D) simplicity — urban
   (E) artificiality — unimaginative

23. If the world is to remain _____ the utmost effort must be made by nations to reduce _____ and to limit local conflicts.

   (A) friendly — diplomacy
   (B) diverse — competition
   (C) industrialized — trade
   (D) healthy — drugs
   (E) peaceful — confrontation

24. She became an ardent abolitionist and in all kinds of tumult and violence, she consistently _____ the _____ of slavery.

   (A) deplored — challengers
   (B) befriended — advocates
   (C) denounced — critics
   (D) attacked — supporters
   (E) evaluated — legitimacy

25. Poe's concern with _____ rather than meaning, his use of suggestiveness rather than _____ gave his stories a unique style and widespread acceptance.

   (A) wordiness — allegory
   (B) imagery — innuendo
   (C) effect — explicitness
   (D) sense — continuity
   (E) incoherence — objectivity

Segment 3: Analogies

Each question below contains a related pair of words or phrases followed by five lettered pairs of words or phrases. Select the answer that best expresses a relationship similar to that expressed in the original pair.

Example:

PURSUE: CATCH::

(A) occur: happen
(B) eat: drink
(C) track: overtake
(D) apprehend: chase
(E) contest: victory

A	B	C	D	E
○	○	●	○	○

26. BEAR: CUB::

    (A) cat: tom   (B) hog: boar
    (C) rabbit: doe   (D) swan: flock
    (E) sheep: lamb

27. MONUMENT: COMMEMORATE::

    (A) prison: parole   (B) palace: rule
    (C) lake: swim   (D) mosque: worship
    (E) park: stroll

28. LICENSE: DRIVING::

    (A) reservation: traveling   (B) university: teaching
    (C) typewriter: writing   (D) registration: voting
    (E) encyclopedia: learning

29. LIBRARIAN: BOOK::

    (A) writer: essay   (B) monk: manuscript
    (C) taxidermist: nature   (D) archivist: document
    (E) actuary: risk

30. LASER: BEAM::

    (A) Loch Ness: monster   (B) limerick: elegy
    (C) loudspeaker: oration   (D) locomotive: steam
    (E) lightning: flash

31. DECIBEL: SOUND::

    (A) eardrum: acoustics   (B) stereo: music
    (C) acre: land   (D) clock: sundial
    (E) moment: minute

32. VICARIOUS: ACTUAL::

    (A) auspicious: unfavorable   (B) perspicuous: clear
    (C) pacifistic: peaceful   (D) ravenous: famished
    (E) clandestine: hidden

33. SAUCE: PIQUANT::

    (A) herb: bitter   (B) butter: rancid
    (C) soup: insipid   (D) appetizer: savory
    (E) steak: satiable

34. SYCOPHANT: FLATTERER::

    (A) gourmet: connoisseur   (B) cavalier: iconoclast
    (C) philanthropist: miser   (D) egotist: ascetic
    (E) orator: demagog

35. COGENT: CONVINCING::

    (A) colloquial: ceremonious   (B) banal: exciting
    (C) culinary: healthy   (D) garrulous: wordy
    (E) militant: complacent

Segment 4: Reading Comprehension

The questions following each passage are based on its content. Your choice should be made on the basis of what is stated *or implied in the passage.*

I got my appointment of course; and I got it very quick. It appears the Company had received news that one of their captains had been killed in a scuffle with the natives.

5 This was my chance, and it made me the more anxious to go. It was only months and months afterwards, when I made the attempt to recover what was left of the body, that I heard the original quarrel

10 arose from a misunderstanding about some hens. Yes, two black hens. Fresleven—that was the fellow's name, a Dane—thought himself wronged somehow in the bargain, so he went ashore and started to hammer the chief

15 of the village with a stick. Oh, it didn't surprise me in the least to hear this, and at the same time to be told that Fresleven was the gentlest, quietest creature that ever walked on two legs. No doubt he was; but he had been

20 a couple of years already out here engaged in the noble cause, you know, and he probably felt the need at last of asserting his self-respect in some way. Therefore he whacked the old man mercilessly, while a big crowd of

25 his people watched him, thunderstruck, till some man—I was told the chief's son—in desperation at hearing the old chap yell, made a tentative jab with a spear—and of course it went quite easy between the shoulder

30 blades. Then the whole population cleared into the forest, expecting all kinds of calamities to happen, while, on the other hand, the steamer Fresleven commanded left also in a bad panic, in charge of the engineer, I be-

35 lieve. Afterwards nobody seemed to trouble much about Fresleven's remains, till I got out and stepped into his shoes. I couldn't let it rest, though; but when an opportunity offered at last to meet my predecessor, the grass

40 growing through his ribs was tall enough to hide his bones. They were all there. The supernatural being had not been touched after he fell. And the village was deserted, the huts gaped black, rotting, all askew within the

45 fallen enclosures. A calamity had come to it, sure enough. The people had vanished. Mad terror had scattered them, men, women, and children, through the bush, and they had never returned. What became of the hens I

50 don't know either. I should think the cause of progress got them, anyhow. However, through this glorious affair I got my appointment,

before I had fairly begun to hope for it.

55 I flew around like mad to get ready, and before forty-eight hours I was crossing the Channel to show myself to my employers, and sign the contract. In a very few hours I arrived in a city that always makes me think of a whited sepulcher*. Prejudice no doubt. I had
60 no difficulty in finding the Company's offices. It was the biggest thing in the town, and everybody I met was full of it. They were going to run an over-sea empire, and make no end of coin by trade.

(Joseph Conrad, *Heart of Darkness*)

*sepulcher—a burial vault

36. It can be inferred from the information in the passage that the speaker has acquired a job as

(A) An engineer on an oil tanker
(B) The captain of a luxury liner
(C) The ambassador to an island republic
(D) The captain of an ocean-going trade ship
(E) The representative of an industrial company

37. According to the passage, Fresleven attacked the native chief because

I. He felt he had been cheated in a business deal
II. He felt the need to declare his self-respect
III. He detested the ignorance of the natives

(A) I only
(C) II only
(E) III only

(B) I and II only
(D) II and III only

38. According to the passage, Fresleven was killed by

(A) The ship's engineer
(C) The Company's representative
(E) The chief's son

(B) The ship's mate
(D) The native chief

39. According to the passage, Fresleven's body was

(A) Carefully hidden by the natives to erase all traces of the incident
(B) Taken aboard ship by the engineer and carried back to civilization
(C) Left undisturbed by the natives
(D) Given a ceremonial burial by the natives
(E) Mutilated by the natives

40. According to the passage, the natives ran into the forest after Fresleven's death because

(A) They felt disaster would strike them because of their role in the incident
(B) They were pursued by Fresleven's crew
(C) The Company had threatened them with violence
(D) They had heard the Company would send a prosecutor to judge them
(E) They had to elect a new chief according to tradition

During the modern period of its history, English has been carried over a large share of the habitable globe, and the number of those who speak it is constantly increasing. Under
5 conditions that existed in former times, this

152

fact could be followed but by one result. Different tongues would have sprung up in different countries, varying from each other, and varying more or less from their common mother; and the differences would have constantly tended to become more marked with the progress of time. But there are two agencies now in existence that will be more than sufficient to prevent any such result. These are, first, the common possession of a great literature accessible to men of every rank and every country; and, secondly, the constant interchange of population that results from the facility of modern communication. Joined to these is the steadily increasing attention paid to the diffusion of education, the direct effect of which is to destroy dialectic differences, and make the literary speech the one standard to which all conform. These agencies become year by year more wide-reaching and controlling. The forces that tend to bring about unity are now so much more powerful than those that tend to bring about diversity, and the former are so constantly gaining in strength, that deviation on any large scale between the language as spoken in Great Britain and in America, can now be looked upon as hardly possible.

What is to be the future of our tongue? Is it steadily tending to become corrupt, as constantly asserted by so many who are laboriously devoting their lives to preserve it in its purity? The fact need not be denied that, within limits, the speech is always moving away from established usage. The history of language is the history of corruptions. The purest of speakers uses every day, with perfect propriety, words and forms, which, looked at from the point of view of the past, are improper, if not scandalous. But the blunders of one age become good usage in the following, and in process of time grow to be so consecrated by custom and consent, that a return to practices theoretically correct would seem like a return to barbarism. While this furnishes no excuse for lax and slovenly methods of expression, it is a guarantee that the indulgence in them by some, or the adoption of them by all will not necessarily be attended by any serious injury to the tongue. Vulgarity and tawdriness and affectation, and numerous other characteristics which are manifested by the users of language, are bad enough; but it is a gross error to suppose that they have of themselves any permanently serious effect upon the purity of national speech. They are

results of imperfect training; and, while the great masters continue to be admired and read and studied, they are results that will last
65 but for a time.
(T. R. Lounsbury, *History of the English Language*)

41. The best title for this passage would be:

    (A) Vulgarities in the English Language
    (B) The Effects of Worldwide Communications
    (C) The English Language: A History
    (D) Education and Language
    (E) The English Language: A Prediction for Its Future

42. According to the passage, the English language will not become fractured into variations because of

    I. Diffusion of education
    II. A common world literature
    III. Modern world communications

    (A) I only   (B) II only
    (C) III only   (D) II and III only
    (E) I, II, and III

43. The tone of the passage can best be described as

    (A) Argumentative   (B) Prejudiced
    (C) Contemplative   (D) Narrative
    (E) Poetic

44. We can infer that the writer would agree with which of the following statements?

    (A) The languages spoken in Great Britain and America are so different that they must be characterized as two distinct languages
    (B) The speakers of the language are ultimately the ones who determine what is good usage
    (C) Vulgarities of language in one age will become accepted, standard usage in another age
    (D) As a result of modern communication systems, different languages will branch off from the English mother tongue
    (E) The English language will tend to become more and more corrupt in time

45. We can infer from the information in the passage that the author is most likely

    (A) A researcher who is interested in discovering the origin of the English language
    (B) An American who idolizes the language as it is spoken in Great Britain
    (C) An historian who is interested in predicting the future of the English language
    (D) A literary critic who is interested in analyzing the influence of great works of literature on the English language
    (E) An educator who is interested in the best way to teach the English language

Section II
Time—30 Minutes

Segment 1: Opposites
Select the word that is most nearly opposite in meaning to the word or phrase in capital letters. Consider any fine shades of meaning that may exist.

Example:

HOT:

    (A) green   (B) river   (C) cold

    (D) above   (E) sweet

A	B	C	D	E
○	○	●	○	○

---

1. SUPERFLUOUS:
   - (A) dangerous
   - (B) malicious
   - (C) necessary
   - (D) favorable
   - (E) small

2. MOROSE:
   - (A) genial
   - (B) stable
   - (C) boring
   - (D) polite
   - (E) audible

3. IRKSOME:
   - (A) insolent
   - (B) gratifying
   - (C) timid
   - (D) forgiving
   - (E) devoted

4. IMPROVIDENT:
   - (A) tolerant
   - (B) prudent
   - (C) irritable
   - (D) fiendish
   - (E) honorable

5. DILATORY:
   - (A) ambitious
   - (B) impatient
   - (C) confident
   - (D) expeditious
   - (E) persistent

6. ACUMEN:
   - (A) adoration
   - (B) hospitality
   - (C) coolheadedness
   - (D) sympathy
   - (E) stupidity

7. PHLEGMATIC:
   - (A) erratic
   - (B) stringent
   - (C) scarce
   - (D) obedient
   - (E) excitable

8. CALUMNY:
   - (A) exaggeration
   - (B) impartiality
   - (C) adulation
   - (D) perfection
   - (E) refinement

155

9. MUNDANE: (A) heavenly   (B) ruddy   (C) inconsequential
                             (D) beneficial   (E) greedy

10. LIBERTINE: (A) prodigy   (B) pirate   (C) prude
                             (D) laborer   (E) misogamist

Segment 2: Sentence Completion

The blanks in each sentence indicate omitted words. Select the word or words that best *fit the meaning of the entire sentence and should be inserted in the blank.*

Example:

On a small farm in an arid climate one should not grow crops that need considerable _____

or _____ to ripen.

(A) fertilizer — attention   (B) space — water
(C) sun — air   (D) tilling — harvesting
(E) weeding — insecticides

                                   A   B   C   D   E
                                   ○ ● ○ ○ ○

---

11. Poor Johnson is not simply _____, he is clearly _____.

   (A) anxious — late   (B) timid — quiet
   (C) upset — distraught   (D) homely — unattractive
   (E) outspoken — curious

12. Evidently disturbed, she tried to cover her _____ by keeping a _____ countenance.

   (A) displeasure — serene   (B) surprise — impertinent
   (C) anguish — tormented   (D) obstinancy — refractory
   (E) fanaticism — savage

13. Prohibition of free speech is a measure so _____ that it would be _____ as the means for

averting a relatively trivial harm to society.

   (A) heinous — befitting   (B) stringent — inappropriate
   (C) arbitrary — admired   (D) unprecedented — unimpeachable
   (E) inconsequential — disregarded

14. An accusation of _____ even when unsupported is often more newsworthy than an expression

of innocence, even when _____.

   (A) murder — justified   (B) incompetence — distasteful
   (C) clumsiness — verified   (D) dissent — disputed
   (E) guilt — documented

15. A successful politician is generally one who is most _____ to his or her _____.

(A) indifferent — community
(B) anonymous — citizenry
(C) devoted — career
(D) obligated — friends
(E) responsive — constituency

Segment 3: Analogies

Each question below contains a related pair of words or phrases followed by five lettered pairs of words or phrases. Select the answer that best expresses a relationship similar to that expressed in the original pair.

Example:
PURSUE: CATCH::

(A) occur: happen
(B) eat: drink
(C) track: overtake
(D) apprehend: chase
(E) contest: victory

	A	B	C	D	E
	○	○	●	○	○

16. OAR: ROWING::

(A) coach: wrestling
(B) sword: fencing
(C) snow: skiing
(D) chalk: bowling
(E) clock: racing

17. CALCULATOR: ACCOUNTANT::

(A) dictation: secretary
(B) snorkle: aviator
(C) sextant: navigator
(D) nursery rhyme: child
(E) stethoscope: orthodontist

18. SLEET: RAIN::

(A) fog: visibility
(B) gust: hurricane
(C) humidity: evaporation
(D) tornado: blizzard
(E) frost: moisture

19. EMBEZZLER: FUNDS::

(A) conspirator: plots
(B) shoplifter: goods
(C) thief: criminal
(D) wastrel: loan
(E) bandit: mask

20. PENICILLIN: BACTERIA::

(A) infection: virus
(B) prognosis: disease
(C) artery: heart
(D) gene: heredity
(E) pesticide: insects

21. CONDUCTOR: ORCHESTRA::

(A) violinist: string section
(B) student: college
(C) marshall: parade
(D) captain: army
(E) guide: pioneers

157

22. ARCHAEOLOGY: ANTIQUITIES::

   (A) pharmacology: aspirin
   (C) embryology: mankind
   (E) geology: continents
   (B) philology: penmanship
   (D) entomology: insects

23. MEAGER: INFINITESIMAL::

   (A) loud: blatant
   (C) buoyant: weighty
   (E) magnanimous: mercenary
   (B) novel: new
   (D) little: miniscule

24. TRUCULENT: CRUEL::

   (A) gregarious: timid
   (C) quixotic: practical
   (E) saturnine: gloomy
   (B) effervescent: distrustful
   (D) egocentric: altruistic

25. ENNUI: BOREDOM::

   (A) credo: belief
   (C) stoicism: enmity
   (E) erudition: scrutiny
   (B) acumen: stupidity
   (D) infirmity: blessing

Segment 4: Reading Comprehension

The questions following each passage are based on its content. Your choice should be made on the basis of what is stated *or implied in the passage.*

The American character is an amalgam of inheritance, environment, and experience. The inheritance is chiefly British, but it is, in a broad sense, that of western Christendom.
5 Contributions from Germany, Scandinavia, Italy, Bohemia, Poland, Russia, and—above all—Africa made an impact on special groups and regions; but their total effect on American institutions was negligible, and only the
10 African had a lasting influence on the American character. The environment, like the inheritance, is varied—varied both in time and in space, for Americans lived in different environments in different eras of their history.
15 The diversity of the environment, however great, was less important than its general character—spaciousness, richness, beauty, and isolation. For over two centuries the environment was a challenge and a reward—
20 a succession of wildernesses that demanded the utmost of those who braved them, and of soils and minerals that rewarded industry and ingenuity richly.

Fully to appreciate the American experi-
25 ence—the third factor in the formation of the national character—would require a rehearsal of the whole of American history. Certain elements of that experience were to prove of special importance to Americans: Puritanism

158

and the principle of the dignity of the
individual; the Enlightenment and the
sovereignty of Reason; the Revolution and
the doctrine of the subordination of government to man; education in self-government
through a constantly expanding electorate and
in democracy through voluntary association;
the absence of feudal institutions of church,
state, and society, and the necessary practice
of social and religious tolerance; freedom from
hard and fast class distinctions; the combina-
tions of abundant natural resources and of
individual industry which made possible a
high level of material prosperity and the
indulgence of women and children; the traditions of immunity from European entangle-
ments, of victory in war, of inexhaustible
resources, of moral superiority, and of Provi-
dential favor—traditions none the less effective even when not consistent with reality.

The Old World inheritance persisted into
the late nineteenth and twentieth centuries,
when it was augmented and, in part, trans-
formed by the new immigration and by the
reception of new scientific and philosophical
ideas such as evolution, determinism, and
Freudianism. With the passing of the frontier
of the nineties the peculiar impact of a wilderness environment disappeared, and as technology enabled man to master their environment, the role of geography and climate was
diminished. Yet the varied forces of weather,
soil, and water, of mountain, prairie, and
forest continued to make themselves felt. A
larger uniformity embraced striking sectional
divergencies, and the American scene presented as richly differentiated an economic
pattern as that of all Europe. And to almost
three centuries of history—often overlaid with
romance or transfigured by legend—Americans added half a century of experience which
by contrast seems almost wholly contem-
poraneous. This recent past, merging imper-
ceptibly with the present, has had a decisive
influence on the shaping of the American
character.
(Henry Steele Commager, *The Meaning of
Reading*)

26. Which of the following titles best summarizes the content of the passage?

(A) America: A Melting Pot
(B) Nature's Influence on the American Character
(C) America's Inheritance
(D) Portrait of the American Character
(E) An Explanation for Democracy

27. The statement that best expresses the writer's main idea is

(A) To understand the distinctiveness of the American, an analysis of the influences of inheritance, environment, and experience is necessary
(B) The recent past, including major technological developments, has had little influence on the shaping of the American character
(C) A study of American history reveals all of the essential factors that have made America what it is today
(D) The diversity in American culture is the result of the different environmental conditions under which Americans live
(E) Although geographically smaller than Europe, America presents a more richly differentiated culture

28. According to the passage, which of the following historical influences have had a major impact on America?

I. Freedom from class distinctions
II. The subordination of government to man
III. Education in self-government

(A) I only   (B) I and II only
(C) II and III only   (D) III only
(E) I, II, and III

29. The effects of geography and climate have diminished in modern America because

(A) Americans have grown more tolerant of nature
(B) American technology has mastered the environment to a great extent
(C) Americans have substituted as a priority the exploration of space
(D) Americans have standardized transportation and communication across the country
(E) Americans have improved scientific meteorological information

30. The author's tone suggests that his attitude toward the study of America is

(A) Casual   (B) Aloof
(C) Analytical   (D) Satiric
(E) Anxious

The most striking and important fact for us is the AFFINITY of the species which inhabit islands closest to those of the nearest mainland, without being actually the same.
5 Numerous instances could be given. The Galapagos Archipelago, situated under the equator, lies at the distance of between 500 and 600 miles from the shores of South America. Here almost every product of the land
10 and of the water bears the unmistakable stamp of the American continent. There are 26 land birds; of these, 21, or perhaps 23 are ranked as distinct species, and would commonly be assumed to have been here
15 created; yet the close affinity of most of these birds to American species is manifest in every character, in their habits, gestures, and tones of voice. So it is with the other animals, and with a large proportion of the plants. The
20 naturalist, looking at the inhabitants of these volcanic islands in the Pacific, distant

160

several hundred miles from the continent, feels that he is standing on American land. Why should this be so? Why should the species which are supposed to have been created in the Galapagos Archipelago, and nowhere else, bear so plainly the stamp of affinity to those created in America? There is nothing in the conditions of life, in the geological nature of the islands, in their height or climate, or in the proportions in which the several classes are associated together, which closely resembles the conditions of the South American coast: in fact, there is a considerable dissimilarity in all these respects. On the other hand, there is a considerable degree of resemblance in the volcanic nature of the soil, in the climate, height, and size of the islands, between the Galapagos and Cape Verde Archipelagoes; but what an entire and absolute difference in their inhabitants! The inhabitants of the Cape Verde Islands are related to those of Africa, like those of the Galapagos to America. Facts such as these admit of no sort of explanation on the ordinary view of independent creation: whereas on the view here maintained, it is obvious that the Galapagos Islands would be likely to receive colonists from America, whether by occasional means of transport or by formerly continuous land, and the Cape Verde Islands from Africa; such colonists would be liable to modification —the principle of inheritance still betraying their original birthplace.

(Charles Darwin, *The Origin of Species*)

31. Which of the following best describes the author's primary purpose in the passage?
    (A) To criticize other scientists
    (B) To describe and hypothesize
    (C) To compare land formations
    (D) To justify established views
    (E) To predict biological trends

32. The author maintains evidence exists to support the view that
    (A) Species of animals and plants are unique to a geographical region
    (B) Species of animals and plants are not greatly influenced by the conditions of life in the areas in which they live
    (C) Species of animals and plants all over the world bear the unmistakable stamp of the American continent
    (D) Species of animals and plants inhabiting islands resemble those species of the nearest mainland
    (E) Species of animals and plants all over the world are direct descendants of those living on the American and African continents

33. According to the passage the Cape Verde Islands are geographically closest to
    (A) South America   (B) North America
    (C) The Equator   (D) Africa
    (E) The Galapagos Archipelago

34. As used in line 2, the word AFFINITY means

(A) Final phase (B) Geographic proximity
(C) Inherent similarity (D) Physical beauty
(E) Number

35. The author suggests that the Galapagos Archipelago and South America may once have been

(A) A continuous land mass
(B) Linked by a chain of islands to Africa
(C) Linked by the Cape Verde Islands
(D) Volcanoes that erupted under the Pacific
(E) Equidistant from the equator

Fundamental to the existence of science is a body of established facts which come either from observation of nature in the raw, so to speak, or from experiment. Without facts we
5 have no science. Facts are to the scientist what words are to the poet. The scientist has a love of facts, even isolated facts, similar to the poet's love of words. But a collection of facts is not science any more than a dic-
10 tionary is poetry. Around his facts that scientist weaves a logical pattern or theory which gives the facts meaning, order, and significance. For example, no one can look at a brilliant night sky without emotion, but the
15 realization that the earth and planets move in great orbits according to simple laws gives proportion and significance to this experience.

Theory may be qualitative and descriptive like Darwin's theory of the origin of species, or
20 quantitative, exact, and mathematical in form like Newton's theory of the motions of planets. In both cases the theory goes far beyond the facts because it has unforeseen consequences which can be applied to new facts or be tested
25 by experiment.

A scientific theory is not a discovery of a law of nature in the sense of a discovery of a mine or the end result of a treasure hunt or a statute that has been hidden in an
30 obscure volume. It is a free creation of a human mind. It becomes a guide to new discovery and a way of looking at the world— which gives it meaning.

A successful theory goes far beyond the facts
35 which it was made to fit. Newton in his laws of motion and theory of universal gravitation essentially created a universe which seemed to have the same properties as the existing universe. But it is hardly to be expected that
40 the creation of a finite human mind would duplicate existing nature in every respect.

162

The history of science indicates that it can't be done. Newton's theory has given place to Einstein's theory of relativity and
45 gravitation. The Darwinian theory has been greatly modified by the geneticists.

The great scientific theories enable us to project our knowledge to enormous distances in time and space. They enable us to pene-
50 trate below the surface to the interior of the atom, or to the operation of our bodies and our minds. They are tremendously strong and beautiful structures, the fruit of the labors of many generations. Yet they are man-made
55 and contingent. New discoveries and insights may modify them or even overthrow them entirely. However, what was good in them is never lost, but is taken over in the new theory in a different context. In this respect the
60 scientist is the most conservative of men.
(I. I. Rabi, *Faith in Science*)

36. Which of the following titles best summarizes the content of the passage?

(A) The Conservative Scientist
(B) Science and Poetry
(C) Theories of Darwin and Newton
(D) Scientific Theory: A Guide to Its Use
(E) Creations of the Human Mind

37. According to the passage, which of the following could be considered "quantitative theories"?

I. Darwin's theory of the origin of the species
II. Newton's theory of the motion of the planets
III. Einstein's theory of relativity and gravitation

(A) I only   (B) II only
(C) III only   (D) I and II only
(E) II and III only

38. In discussing the application of facts to scientific theory the writer uses

I. Analogy
II. Illustration
III. Statistics

(A) I only   (B) II only
(C) I and II only   (D) III only
(E) I, II, and III

39. According to the passage, a successful scientific theory

(A) Goes beyond the facts   (B) Requires great mental ability
(C) Contains poetic language   (D) Duplicates nature
(E) Rarely changes

40. According to the passage, all of the following describe scientific theories <u>except</u>

(A) They are strong and beautiful structures
(B) They are man-made and contingent
(C) They are discoveries of nature's laws
(D) They are creations of a finite mind
(E) They are tested by experiment

Answer Sheet
for
Simulated Verbal Examination

Number One

Segment 1: Opposites

	A	B	C	D	E
1.	○	○	○	○	○
2.	○	○	○	○	○
3.	○	○	○	○	○
4.	○	○	○	○	○
5.	○	○	○	○	○
6.	○	○	○	○	○
7.	○	○	○	○	○
8.	○	○	○	○	○
9.	○	○	○	○	○
10.	○	○	○	○	○
11.	○	○	○	○	○
12.	○	○	○	○	○
13.	○	○	○	○	○
14.	○	○	○	○	○
15.	○	○	○	○	○

Segment 3: Analogies

	A	B	C	D	E
26.	○	○	○	○	○
27.	○	○	○	○	○
28.	○	○	○	○	○
29.	○	○	○	○	○
30.	○	○	○	○	○
31.	○	○	○	○	○
32.	○	○	○	○	○
33.	○	○	○	○	○
34.	○	○	○	○	○
35.	○	○	○	○	○

Segment 2: Sentence Completion

	A	B	C	D	E
16.	○	○	○	○	○
17.	○	○	○	○	○
18.	○	○	○	○	○
19.	○	○	○	○	○
20.	○	○	○	○	○
21.	○	○	○	○	○
22.	○	○	○	○	○
23.	○	○	○	○	○
24.	○	○	○	○	○
25.	○	○	○	○	○

Segment 4: Reading Comprehension

	A	B	C	D	E
36.	○	○	○	○	○
37.	○	○	○	○	○
38.	○	○	○	○	○
39.	○	○	○	○	○
40.	○	○	○	○	○
41.	○	○	○	○	○
42.	○	○	○	○	○
43.	○	○	○	○	○
44.	○	○	○	○	○
45.	○	○	○	○	○

Answer Sheet
for
Simulated Verbal Examination

Number Two

Segment 1: Opposites

	A	B	C	D	E
1.	○	○	○	○	○
2.	○	○	○	○	○
3.	○	○	○	○	○
4.	○	○	○	○	○
5.	○	○	○	○	○
6.	○	○	○	○	○
7.	○	○	○	○	○
8.	○	○	○	○	○
9.	○	○	○	○	○
10.	○	○	○	○	○

Segment 2: Sentence Completion

	A	B	C	D	E
11.	○	○	○	○	○
12.	○	○	○	○	○
13.	○	○	○	○	○
14.	○	○	○	○	○
15.	○	○	○	○	○

Segment 3: Analogies

	A	B	C	D	E
16.	○	○	○	○	○
17.	○	○	○	○	○
18.	○	○	○	○	○
19.	○	○	○	○	○
20.	○	○	○	○	○
21.	○	○	○	○	○
22.	○	○	○	○	○
23.	○	○	○	○	○
24.	○	○	○	○	○
25.	○	○	○	○	○

Segment 4: Reading Comprehension

	A	B	C	D	E
26.	○	○	○	○	○
27.	○	○	○	○	○
28.	○	○	○	○	○
29.	○	○	○	○	○
30.	○	○	○	○	○
31.	○	○	○	○	○
32.	○	○	○	○	○
33.	○	○	○	○	○
34.	○	○	○	○	○
35.	○	○	○	○	○
36.	○	○	○	○	○
37.	○	○	○	○	○
38.	○	○	○	○	○
39.	○	○	○	○	○
40.	○	○	○	○	○

Answer Sheet
for
Simulated Verbal Examination

Number Three

Segment 1: Opposites

	A	B	C	D	E
1.	○	○	○	○	○
2.	○	○	○	○	○
3.	○	○	○	○	○
4.	○	○	○	○	○
5.	○	○	○	○	○
6.	○	○	○	○	○
7.	○	○	○	○	○
8.	○	○	○	○	○
9.	○	○	○	○	○
10.	○	○	○	○	○
11.	○	○	○	○	○
12.	○	○	○	○	○
13.	○	○	○	○	○
14.	○	○	○	○	○
15.	○	○	○	○	○

Segment 3: Analogies

	A	B	C	D	E
26.	○	○	○	○	○
27.	○	○	○	○	○
28.	○	○	○	○	○
29.	○	○	○	○	○
30.	○	○	○	○	○
31.	○	○	○	○	○
32.	○	○	○	○	○
33.	○	○	○	○	○
34.	○	○	○	○	○
35.	○	○	○	○	○

Segment 2: Sentence Completion

	A	B	C	D	E
16.	○	○	○	○	○
17.	○	○	○	○	○
18.	○	○	○	○	○
19.	○	○	○	○	○
20.	○	○	○	○	○
21.	○	○	○	○	○
22.	○	○	○	○	○
23.	○	○	○	○	○
24.	○	○	○	○	○
25.	○	○	○	○	○

Segment 4: Reading Comprehension

	A	B	C	D	E
36.	○	○	○	○	○
37.	○	○	○	○	○
38.	○	○	○	○	○
39.	○	○	○	○	○
40.	○	○	○	○	○
41.	○	○	○	○	○
42.	○	○	○	○	○
43.	○	○	○	○	○
44.	○	○	○	○	○
45.	○	○	○	○	○

Answer Sheet
for
Simulated Verbal Examination

Number Four

Segment 1: Opposites

	A	B	C	D	E
1.	○	○	○	○	○
2.	○	○	○	○	○
3.	○	○	○	○	○
4.	○	○	○	○	○
5.	○	○	○	○	○
6.	○	○	○	○	○
7.	○	○	○	○	○
8.	○	○	○	○	○
9.	○	○	○	○	○
10.	○	○	○	○	○

Segment 2: Sentence Completion

	A	B	C	D	E
11.	○	○	○	○	○
12.	○	○	○	○	○
13.	○	○	○	○	○
14.	○	○	○	○	○
15.	○	○	○	○	○

Segment 3: Analogies

	A	B	C	D	E
16.	○	○	○	○	○
17.	○	○	○	○	○
18.	○	○	○	○	○
19.	○	○	○	○	○
20.	○	○	○	○	○
21.	○	○	○	○	○
22.	○	○	○	○	○
23.	○	○	○	○	○
24.	○	○	○	○	○
25.	○	○	○	○	○

Segment 4: Reading Comprehension

	A	B	C	D	E
26.	○	○	○	○	○
27.	○	○	○	○	○
28.	○	○	○	○	○
29.	○	○	○	○	○
30.	○	○	○	○	○
31.	○	○	○	○	○
32.	○	○	○	○	○
33.	○	○	○	○	○
34.	○	○	○	○	○
35.	○	○	○	○	○
36.	○	○	○	○	○
37.	○	○	○	○	○
38.	○	○	○	○	○
39.	○	○	○	○	○
40.	○	○	○	○	○

Answer Sheet
for
Simulated Verbal Examination

Number Five

Segment 1: Opposites

	A	B	C	D	E
1.	○	○	○	○	○
2.	○	○	○	○	○
3.	○	○	○	○	○
4.	○	○	○	○	○
5.	○	○	○	○	○
6.	○	○	○	○	○
7.	○	○	○	○	○
8.	○	○	○	○	○
9.	○	○	○	○	○
10.	○	○	○	○	○

Segment 2: Sentence Completion

	A	B	C	D	E
11.	○	○	○	○	○
12.	○	○	○	○	○
13.	○	○	○	○	○
14.	○	○	○	○	○
15.	○	○	○	○	○

Segment 3: Analogies

	A	B	C	D	E
16.	○	○	○	○	○
17.	○	○	○	○	○
18.	○	○	○	○	○
19.	○	○	○	○	○
20.	○	○	○	○	○
21.	○	○	○	○	○
22.	○	○	○	○	○
23.	○	○	○	○	○
24.	○	○	○	○	○
25.	○	○	○	○	○

Segment 4: Reading Comprehension

	A	B	C	D	E
26.	○	○	○	○	○
27.	○	○	○	○	○
28.	○	○	○	○	○
29.	○	○	○	○	○
30.	○	○	○	○	○
31.	○	○	○	○	○
32.	○	○	○	○	○
33.	○	○	○	○	○
34.	○	○	○	○	○
35.	○	○	○	○	○
36.	○	○	○	○	○
37.	○	○	○	○	○
38.	○	○	○	○	○
39.	○	○	○	○	○
40.	○	○	○	○	○

Answer Sheet
for
Simulated Test of Standard Written English

Test I

Part I

	A	B	C	D	E
1.	○	○	○	○	○
2.	○	○	○	○	○
3.	○	○	○	○	○
4.	○	○	○	○	○
5.	○	○	○	○	○
6.	○	○	○	○	○
7.	○	○	○	○	○
8.	○	○	○	○	○
9.	○	○	○	○	○
10.	○	○	○	○	○
11.	○	○	○	○	○
12.	○	○	○	○	○
13.	○	○	○	○	○
14.	○	○	○	○	○
15.	○	○	○	○	○
16.	○	○	○	○	○
17.	○	○	○	○	○
18.	○	○	○	○	○
19.	○	○	○	○	○
20.	○	○	○	○	○
21.	○	○	○	○	○
22.	○	○	○	○	○
23.	○	○	○	○	○
24.	○	○	○	○	○
25.	○	○	○	○	○

Part II

	A	B	C	D	E
26.	○	○	○	○	○
27.	○	○	○	○	○
28.	○	○	○	○	○
29.	○	○	○	○	○
30.	○	○	○	○	○
31.	○	○	○	○	○
32.	○	○	○	○	○
33.	○	○	○	○	○
34.	○	○	○	○	○
35.	○	○	○	○	○
36.	○	○	○	○	○
37.	○	○	○	○	○
38.	○	○	○	○	○
39.	○	○	○	○	○
40.	○	○	○	○	○

Part III

	A	B	C	D	E
41.	○	○	○	○	○
42.	○	○	○	○	○
43.	○	○	○	○	○
44.	○	○	○	○	○
45.	○	○	○	○	○
46.	○	○	○	○	○
47.	○	○	○	○	○
48.	○	○	○	○	○
49.	○	○	○	○	○
50.	○	○	○	○	○

Answer Sheet
for
Simulated Test of Standard Written English

Test II

Part I

	A	B	C	D	E
1.	○	○	○	○	○
2.	○	○	○	○	○
3.	○	○	○	○	○
4.	○	○	○	○	○
5.	○	○	○	○	○
6.	○	○	○	○	○
7.	○	○	○	○	○
8.	○	○	○	○	○
9.	○	○	○	○	○
10.	○	○	○	○	○
11.	○	○	○	○	○
12.	○	○	○	○	○
13.	○	○	○	○	○
14.	○	○	○	○	○
15.	○	○	○	○	○
16.	○	○	○	○	○
17.	○	○	○	○	○
18.	○	○	○	○	○
19.	○	○	○	○	○
20.	○	○	○	○	○
21.	○	○	○	○	○
22.	○	○	○	○	○
23.	○	○	○	○	○
24.	○	○	○	○	○
25.	○	○	○	○	○

Part II

	A	B	C	D	E
26.	○	○	○	○	○
27.	○	○	○	○	○
28.	○	○	○	○	○
29.	○	○	○	○	○
30.	○	○	○	○	○
31.	○	○	○	○	○
32.	○	○	○	○	○
33.	○	○	○	○	○
34.	○	○	○	○	○
35.	○	○	○	○	○
36.	○	○	○	○	○
37.	○	○	○	○	○
38.	○	○	○	○	○
39.	○	○	○	○	○
40.	○	○	○	○	○

Part III

	A	B	C	D	E
41.	○	○	○	○	○
42.	○	○	○	○	○
43.	○	○	○	○	○
44.	○	○	○	○	○
45.	○	○	○	○	○
46.	○	○	○	○	○
47.	○	○	○	○	○
48.	○	○	○	○	○
49.	○	○	○	○	○
50.	○	○	○	○	○

Answer Sheet
for
Comprehensive Simulated Verbal Examination

Section I

Segment 1: Opposites

	A	B	C	D	E
1.	○	○	○	○	○
2.	○	○	○	○	○
3.	○	○	○	○	○
4.	○	○	○	○	○
5.	○	○	○	○	○
6.	○	○	○	○	○
7.	○	○	○	○	○
8.	○	○	○	○	○
9.	○	○	○	○	○
10.	○	○	○	○	○
11.	○	○	○	○	○
12.	○	○	○	○	○
13.	○	○	○	○	○
14.	○	○	○	○	○
15.	○	○	○	○	○

Segment 3: Analogies

	A	B	C	D	E
26.	○	○	○	○	○
27.	○	○	○	○	○
28.	○	○	○	○	○
29.	○	○	○	○	○
30.	○	○	○	○	○
31.	○	○	○	○	○
32.	○	○	○	○	○
33.	○	○	○	○	○
34.	○	○	○	○	○
35.	○	○	○	○	○

Segment 2: Sentence Completion

	A	B	C	D	E
16.	○	○	○	○	○
17.	○	○	○	○	○
18.	○	○	○	○	○
19.	○	○	○	○	○
20.	○	○	○	○	○
21.	○	○	○	○	○
22.	○	○	○	○	○
23.	○	○	○	○	○
24.	○	○	○	○	○
25.	○	○	○	○	○

Segment 4: Reading Comprehension

	A	B	C	D	E
36.	○	○	○	○	○
37.	○	○	○	○	○
38.	○	○	○	○	○
39.	○	○	○	○	○
40.	○	○	○	○	○
41.	○	○	○	○	○
42.	○	○	○	○	○
43.	○	○	○	○	○
44.	○	○	○	○	○
45.	○	○	○	○	○

Answer Sheet
for
Comprehensive Simulated Verbal Examination

Section II

Segment 1: Opposites

	A	B	C	D	E
1.	○	○	○	○	○
2.	○	○	○	○	○
3.	○	○	○	○	○
4.	○	○	○	○	○
5.	○	○	○	○	○
6.	○	○	○	○	○
7.	○	○	○	○	○
8.	○	○	○	○	○
9.	○	○	○	○	○
10.	○	○	○	○	○

Segment 2: Sentence Completion

	A	B	C	D	E
11.	○	○	○	○	○
12.	○	○	○	○	○
13.	○	○	○	○	○
14.	○	○	○	○	○
15.	○	○	○	○	○

Segment 3: Analogies

	A	B	C	D	E
16.	○	○	○	○	○
17.	○	○	○	○	○
18.	○	○	○	○	○
19.	○	○	○	○	○
20.	○	○	○	○	○
21.	○	○	○	○	○
22.	○	○	○	○	○
23.	○	○	○	○	○
24.	○	○	○	○	○
25.	○	○	○	○	○

Segment 4: Reading Comprehension

	A	B	C	D	E
26.	○	○	○	○	○
27.	○	○	○	○	○
28.	○	○	○	○	○
29.	○	○	○	○	○
30.	○	○	○	○	○
31.	○	○	○	○	○
32.	○	○	○	○	○
33.	○	○	○	○	○
34.	○	○	○	○	○
35.	○	○	○	○	○
36.	○	○	○	○	○
37.	○	○	○	○	○
38.	○	○	○	○	○
39.	○	○	○	○	○
40.	○	○	○	○	○